Copycat Recipes

A step by step guide for making the most famous tasty restaurant dishes at home.

With 2 manuscripts: Copycat Recipes Cookbook, Keto Copycat Recipes.

With recipes for the keto diet

Lisa Ramsey

Table of Contents

Copycat Recipes Cookbook

Keto Copycat Recipes

Copycat Recipes Cookbook

Learn to make 82 of your most famous restaurants' copycat recipes at home

Lisa Ramsey

Introduction

An exciting journey awaits you on this read! Get ready to learn some tasty, fantastically easy and fun recipes for all times of the day. And the little cherry on top? We've added in some scrumptious special recipes that will taste just like your favorite restaurant meals!

As vital as food is, there are so many exciting elements that contribute to what makes food a *meal*! And that is exactly what you will discover in this read – you will begin to understand and truly appreciate recipes, from their story to the aroma, culture, history, flavor, nutritional value, and most importantly, how it affects your mind and emotions! Cooking, in itself, is extremely therapeutic – from practicing the art of self-love, whereby you put in the time and effort to learn and whip up a delicious meal for yourself/friends and family, to discovering how beneficial the role of a good diet can play in our lives. Cooking in itself is a memory, a form of therapy and you learn an amazing and vital skill set along the way!

Copycat Recipes will also give you some sneaky inside tips on how to comfort your cravings for some of your favorite takeaway/restaurant spots and show you just how easy it will be to make homemade versions, as well as have a good amount of food for cost factor involved (not to mention the rewarding feeling will make the meal taste so much better)!

We have included a wonderful variety of meals within one simple recipe book so that all your possible meal preps/cravings are catered to! You will notice a vast array of recipes ranging from healthy breakfasts to Portuguese seafood cuisines, from fast food styled crumb chicken to New York deep dish pasta – yes, all of these recipes are at the tips of your fingers and ready for you to make some lovely home cooked meals with! So get your best apron on and get ready to travel the world with *Copycat Recipes*, from the comfort of your own home!

Well, read this book now and don't forget to let me know what you think whit a short review if you enjoy it. Thanks!

Chapter 1: Breakfast

Breakfast definitely is the most important part of our day, as you ensure that your body is getting the right kind of nutrition and energy it needs for it to wake up and have the most productive day! Consuming a good breakfast will help your body and mind re-energize and endure through a more productive day without tiring out too quickly; in this chapter, you'll get to explore some delicious options of breakfasts - from smoothie bowls to scrumptious English breakfasts, the variety of listed meal options will all guarantee you have a happy and healthy body!

Whole Wheat Pancakes

From berries to bacon: Pancakes work well with everything! So, it only seems fair to start off this breakfast list with a simple yet wholesome pancake recipe. This specific recipe is a little healthier than the usual pancake recipe, as it doesn't require butter at all! Your pancakes will still be fluffy and scrumptious, while still leaving you feeling fulfilled and energized from the nutrition!

Prep Time: 15 minutes

Cooking Time: 20 minutes

Nutritional Facts/Info:		
9-10 Pancakes/Servings	Per Serving	% Daily Value
Calories	235	
Carbs	36g	13%
Fat	7.2g	9%
Protein	6g	

Ingredients:

- 1 ½ cups of milk (alternatively you can use oat/soy milk)
- ¼ cup of white vinegar
- 2 large free-range eggs
- ¼ cup of oil
- ¼ cup of honey (golden/maple syrup is also a good substitute)
- 2 ½ cups of whole wheat flour
- 1 tsp baking soda
- 1 tsp baking powder
- 1 tsp cinnamon
- ¼ salt

- oil (or butter) to lightly grease your pan

Directions:

1. Pour the vinegar and milk into a bowl and gently stir the mixture. Leave the mixture to stand for about 10 minutes – it should start to curdle and become "buttermilk".
2. While you allow the mixture to stand, you can preheat your pan to a medium-high heat.
3. Whisk the eggs, oil, honey, baking soda, baking powder, cinnamon and salt into your buttermilk mixture, making sure it is well combined.
4. Gently sift the flour into the mixture and stir well with a spatula/wooden spoon, breaking down all the lumps.
5. Once your pan is hot enough, lightly drizzle some oil/butter to evenly coat the surface of the pan (make sure the oil sizzles, so your pancakes can fry nicely).
6. Using a spoon/cup, pour your mixture into the pan, creating circular shapes – you can decide how big/small you'd like your pancakes to be. Allow the mixture to fry for 3-4 minutes (you should start seeing bubbles appear in the mixture or browning around the circumference). Flip the pancakes and cook for another minute.
7. Repeat the process until your batter is done – remember to adjust the heat of your pan accordingly:

Since the oil is now hot, it may burn your pancakes if you leave the heat on too high.

Voila! You've made perfect, fluffy and healthy pancakes that will keep you feeling full! You can add your own touches of green yogurt, honey, berries – whatever you fancy for that day! If you have any leftovers, you can always pop them in the freezer and reheat them out throughout the week!

Dark Chocolate & Cinnamon Quinoa Bowl

Breakfast bowls have grown popular over the recent years – they're easy to whip up, healthy, filling and well-balanced meals! It's a great way to start your morning off. Though there are so many possibilities of what breakfast bowls could consist of, the tastiest and simultaneously healthy bowl has got to be the quinoa and dark chocolate breakfast bowl – it promises a sweet, cocoa treat while giving you an incredible energy boost!

Prep Time: 5 minutes

Cooking Time: 25 minutes

Nutritional Facts/Info:		
4 Servings	Per Serving	
Calories	473	
Carbs	52.8g	19%
Fat	29.4g	38%
Protein	11.2g	

Ingredients:

- 1 cup of uncooked quinoa
- 1 cup of almond milk (alternatively you can use soy/oat/rice milk)
- 1 cup of coconut milk
- a pinch of salt
- a pinch of cinnamon
- 2 tbsp of cocoa powder
- 2-3 tbsp of honey
- 3-4 squares of dark chocolate
- 1 banana
- a handful of raisins/berries (optional)

Directions:

1. Place a pan on medium heat.

2. While the pan heats up, rinse your quinoa for about 2 minutes and then strain it out.

3. Pour the washed quinoa into the pan and allow it to slightly toast.

4. Add your almond milk, coconut milk, and salt into the pot and slowly mix the ingredients together. Raise the heat and bring to boil, then lower the heat, allowing the pot to simmer for about 20-25 minutes, stirring frequently.

5. Once the quinoa has absorbed the liquid, remove the pot from the hot plate and mix in your cocoa powder, honey and cinnamon. You can add in more almond milk if you'd fancy a more milky texture.

6. Chop up your banana and chocolate squares and mix them into your bowl. Add raisins/berries if you have any.

7. You can refrigerate the quinoa for up to 2-3 days if you have any leftovers, and add in more almond milk when reheating it, to bring back the moistness.

A Berry French Toast

The best part about French Toast is that, just like pancakes, it is super versatile in what you can add to it. But for this recipe, we'll be adding our own twist by incorporating it with delicious berries and yogurt! You not only get the benefit of good protein, you also comfort your sweet tooth craving by getting in on some zesty berry action!

Prep Time: 5 minutes

Cooking Time: 15 minutes

Nutritional Facts/Info:		
1 Serving	Per Serving	
Calories	128	
Carbs	7.9g	3%
Fat	7.2g	9%
Protein	6.1g	

Ingredients:

- 2 free-range eggs
- ¼ cup milk
- ½ tbsp vanilla extract
- a pinch of cinnamon
- a pinch of salt
- a pinch of mixed herbs/rosemary
- 2 slices of bread (multi seed/rye is preferred)
- olive oil or butter, to grease the pan

- Greek yogurt (for serving)
- Honey/maple syrup (for drizzling)
- a handful of berries (you can use other fruits like apples, banana, pineapple if you desire)

Directions:

1. Crack the eggs into a bowl and then pour in the milk, vanilla extract, cinnamon and salt. Whisk the ingredients together until you see a lovely froth surfacing.
2. Soak the bread in the mixture, gently pressing on them, and turn the slices after a few minutes (the longer the bread soaks, the better).
3. While your bread is soaking in the mix, heat up your frying pan and lightly coat the base of the pan with olive oil/butter.
4. Once the pan is heated and the oil is sizzling, place your bread slices in the pan and toast. Flip them over after a few minutes to toast the other side.
5. Once the slices are toasted, plate them with a few spoons of Greek yogurt and berries. Drizzle your honey/maple syrup over it and perfecto, you have your own berry french toast!

Eggs Benedict with Hollandaise Sauce

As fancy as it sounds, preparing a perfect Eggs Benedict is much simpler than it seems! To top it off, we've also included a divine, tangy, homemade Hollandaise sauce recipe which pairs perfectly with your Eggs Benedict, so that you get the entire brunch experience right at home!

Prep Time: 5 minutes

Cooking Time: 20 minutes

Nutritional Facts/Info:		
4 Servings	Per Serving	
Calories	413	
Carbs	14g	5%
Fat	28.3g	36%
Protein	24.2g	

Ingredients:

- 8 rashes of bacon
- 4 eggs
- 2 tsp of white vinegar

- 2 English muffins (you can substitute this for other carbs, like rye bread, scones, bagels, etc.)
- 1 ½ tsp of butter

Hollandaise Sauce:

- 5 tbsp unsalted butter (if you have salted butter, omit the salt from this recipe)
- 3 egg yolks
- 1 tbsp of lemon juice
- ½ tsp salt
- dash of cayenne pepper or tabasco

Directions:

1. Preheat a frying pan on medium heat for your bacon and add a drizzle of oil. Preheat another medium saucepan filled 2/3 up with water to a boil, for your eggs. Once the water is boiling, add in your vinegar and then lower the heat so it begins to simmer.

2. Place your bacon strips in the frying pan and allow them to fry for about 10 minutes (until crispy brown). While your bacon is frying, crack one egg into the saucepan with water and wait for it to solidify a little. Once you can see the egg starting to gain a nice white circular form, you can add another. Repeat the process until all your eggs are in the pot, then lower the heat

and cover the pot with a lid and let it cook for about 4 minutes.

3. Prep your English muffins – you can either toast them or butter them up. If you prefer a nice greasy breakfast – you can use the same pan that you fried your bacon in, to toast your muffins/bread. It brings a lovely flavor to the muffins, and you save on oil.

4. Check on your bacon to see if it's crisp – once it is, remove it with a fork and place it on a paper towel (this drains out the excess fat) with a plate under it.

5. Once your eggs have been cooking for about 4 minutes, gently scoop them out with a sieve or a slotted spoon, so that you drain out excess water and place them over the english muffins.

6. Now for the Hollandaise sauce: melt your 5 tbsp of butter. In a blender (if you don't have a blender, you can whisk these ingredients together), combine the 3 egg yolks, lemon juice, cayenne and salt and blend for 20 seconds until the mixture looks a light pale yellow in color. Then lower your mixing speed, and drizzle in your butter.

7. Once mixed, dollop the Hollandaise sauce over your eggs and serve with bacon.

Feta Frittata

Originated in Italy, a 'Frittata' is similar to a quiche, but without the crust. They are incredibly versatile as once you master the basic recipe of it, you can add hundreds of different ingredients and combinations to make it your own!

Prep Time: 5 minutes

Cooking Time: 15 minutes

Nutritional Facts/Info:		
4 Servings	Per Serving	
Calories	163	
Carbs	6.4g	2%
Fat	10g	13%
Protein	12.9g	

Ingredients:

- 6 eggs
- ¼ cup of milk
- 2 garlic cloves/1 tsp garlic paste
- ¼ tsp salt & ¼ tsp pepper

- ½ tsp chilli flakes
- ¼ onion, chopped
- 2 scallions, diced
- 2 cups of broccoli
- ¼ cup of Feta cheese
- a handful of seeds (optional)
- 1 tbsp oil

Directions:

1. Drizzle the oil into a small pan over medium heat. Toss in your onions, scallions, chilli flakes, and salt and pepper, and fry them.
2. In a separate bowl, combine your eggs, milk, garlic, and a pinch of salt and pepper, and whisk well.
3. Preheat your oven to 400°F and lightly grease a baking dish (8x8 dish is best suited).
4. Once the onions in the pan begin to brown a little, add in your broccoli and cook for about 5 minutes – then slowly pour the egg mixture into the pan, add in some seeds and lightly stir, just to even out the contents.
5. Next, pour the contents from the pan into the baking dish and crumble Feta cheese over the top.
6. Pop the dish in the oven and bake for 20 minutes.

Savory Muffins

Muffins are never not a good idea – they're easy to whip up, you can ensure that you have a few for the week and they're great to grab if you're on the run and need a quick bite!

P.S these muffins are quite high in protein and low in carbs, so they're especially great for a post-workout snack!

Prep Time: 10 minutes

Cooking Time: 15 minutes

Nutritional Facts/Info:		
6 Muffins	Per Serving	
Calories	197	
Carbs	4.5g	2%
Fat	14.2g	18%
Protein	13.6g	

Ingredients:

- 4 eggs
- 200g spinach

- ¼ tomato
- ½ cup of mixed veg stir fry or alternatively):
    - ¼ cup of corn
    - ¼ cup of peas
    - 100g green beans
    - ¼ red onion
- 200g cheddar cheese
- 1 tsp salt
- 1 tsp cayenne pepper
- ½ tsp chilli flakes
- 1 tsp garlic & herb paste
- 1 tbsp olive oil
- 1 tbsp butter

Directions:

1. Drizzle olive oil into a skillet/pan over medium heat.
2. Dice the tomato, cheese and onion and finely chop the spinach and green beans.
3. Use the butter to grease a muffin tray and preheat your oven to 400° F.
4. Crack the eggs into the pan, add your salt, pepper, chilli flakes and garlic & herb paste and carefully whisk the mixture together until light and fluffy.
5. Add in all the vegetables and cheese and give the mixture one last stir, before evenly pouring the mixture

into 6 of the cups in the muffin tray – each cup should be about ¾ filled with mixture.

6. Pop the tray in the oven and bake for 15 - 20 minutes.

Smoothie Bowl

Smoothie bowls are another form of breakfast that's gained incredible popularity over the years – it's a great source of getting your vitamin boost (of fruit and veggies) in for the day and it will also leave you feeling energized and full!

Prep Time: 5 minutes

Cooking Time: 2 minutes

Nutritional Facts/Info:		
1 Serving	per serving	
Calories	641	
Carbs	112.3g	41%
Fat	25.1g	32%
Protein	7.4g	

Ingredients:

- 1 ½ cups of frozen mango (alternatively, ½ a normal mango, chopped)
- 2 bananas
- ¼ avocado
- 1 tbsp lemon juice
- ¼ almond milk
- 2 dates
- 4 strawberries
- 1 tsp cinnamon

Directions:

1. Pour your liquids into a blender and then add in your solid ingredients. Blend until smooth.
2. Pour into a bowl and enjoy!

Green Detox Smoothie

Some mornings need a little stronger kickstarter than others - you may be feeling a little lethargic, fluey, or maybe even a little bloated or nauseous. Whatever the case may be, a good detox drink every now and then is a great gift to your body! This fantastic green juice will give you all the wonderful vitamins, probiotics and organic energy boost that you need for those more challenging days!

Prep Time: 2 minutes

Cooking Time: 2 minutes

Nutritional Facts/Info:		
1 Serving	Per Serving	
Calories	401	
Carbs	91.6g	33%
Fat	5.2g	7%
Protein	6.9g	

Ingredients:

- 3 cups of spinach (rinsed out)
- 1 banana
- 1 granny smith apple
- ⅓ cucumber
- 10g of mint
- 4 dates
- 1 tbsp flax seeds
- ½ cup of almond milk
- 1 tsp lemon juice
- ½ tsp honey

Directions:

1. Finely chop/dice your spinach, banana, apple, mint and dates.
2. Combine all the ingredients into a blender, starting with your liquids first.

NY Style Bagels

And after all those lovely vitamin boost smoothie ideas, it's time to dig into some juicy New York inspired bagels, which are tantalizingly filled with cheese, greasy bacon, delicious fried eggs and butter! The aroma alone will have your tummy growling to eagerly munch away. The best part is that it only requires a few ingredients, yet it tastes and smells *heavenly*!

Prep Time: 2 minutes

Cooking Time: 10 minutes

Nutritional Facts/Info:		
1 Bagel Sandwich	Per Serving	
Calories	921	
Carbs	33.2g	12%

Fat	70.7g	91%
Protein	38.9g	

Ingredients:

- 1 bagel
- 3 tablespoons of butter
- 2 rashers of bacon
- 2 eggs
- 2 slices of cheddar/mozzarella
- ¼ cup of raw spinach
- salt, mixed herb spice & pepper to taste

Directions:

1. Preheat a pan over medium heat and rinse out your spinach whilst the pan heats up.
2. Halve your bagel and butter on either side and place it on the pan to toast till crisp, golden brown. To save on time, you can also add your rashers of bacon to the pan so it can fry.
3. Once the bagel and bagel are done, place them on the side and add another spoon of butter into the pan, then crack both eggs into the pan. When the egg whites start to solidify, puncture the egg yolks with a fork and

spread the yolk evenly over the egg whites and then sprinkle some salt and pepper over them.

4. Place the cheese and bacon on top of the eggs and, using a spatula, flip the eggs over, allowing it to fry for another minute.

5. Transfer the glorious egg-bacon-cheese patty onto your bagel and place the spinach in. Serve while as warm as possible.

Avocado & Poached Eggs on Toast

Lastly, we can't ignore the massive trendsetting recipe that has taken the young hipsters by storm: avocado toast! We've included some scrambled eggs on the side to make it more of a filling meal, but you can definitely enjoy it plain for breakfast, or as a quick snack!

Prep Time: 5 minutes

Cooking Time: 10 minutes

Nutritional Facts/Info:		
1 Serving	Per Serving	
Calories	393	

Carbs	30.1g	11%
Fat	20.4g	26%
Protein	23.3g	47%

Ingredients:

- 2 eggs
- ½ an avocado
- 50g of feta cheese
- 2 slices of rye bread
- salt, pepper, mixed herbs, turmeric (for seasoning, a pinch of each is fine)
- 2 tbsp of milk
- 1 tbsp oil
- a squeeze of lemon juice
- Tabasco sauce (if you'd like a kick of spice)
- a handful of seeds (sunflower is best)
- a handful of baby tomatoes for a side serving

Directions:

1. Bring a medium pan to a low-medium heat on the stove and drizzle a little oil in it.
2. Crack the eggs into the pot and sprinkle a pinch of salt, pepper, mixed herbs. Pour in your milk and stir the

mixture with a fork/whisk ensuring that the yolks break apart and the entire mixture is a pale yellow.

3. While the eggs cook, pop your slices of rye bread in the toaster.

4. As the mixture starts to solidify, continue mixing every once in a while to break up the mixture. Once the eggs have fully cooked (it'll look golden yellow and chunky), take them off the heat.

5. Slice your avocado lengthwise and evenly spread it over the toasted rye. Sprinkle some salt and turmeric and squeeze some lemon juice over the avocados, then add your scrambled eggs on top.

6. Crumble some feta cheese over the top and then sprinkle sunflower seeds over. Dash a bit of tabasco sauce if you'd like a little spicy kick.

7. Halve your tomatoes and serve it on the side, next to your avocado toast!

Chapter 2: Appetizers

Appetizers are light, flavorful snacks or finger foods that are consumed in anticipation of the meal that is to come. They set the atmosphere and theme for the meal, and are mainly used to entertain guests while they mingle and await the main course.

1. Caramel Cream Cheese Spread

This recipe is super quick to put together and requires extremely little cooking! If you need a light snack that's perfect for any time of day, this perfect sweet and savory treat is a great option.

Prep Time: 5 minutes

Cooking Time: 10 minutes

Nutritional Facts/Info:		
12 Servings	Per Serving	
Calories	116	
Carbs	7.8g	3%

Fat	9g	11%
Protein	1.5g	

Ingredients:

- 8 oz of cream cheese
- ½ a cup of toffee bits
- 5 sliced apples, pears & pretzels for serving
- 1 cup of brown sugar
- 6 tbsp of salted butter, cubed
- ½ cup of whipped cream
- pinch of cinnamon

Directions:

1. Pour the sugar into a saucepan over medium heat and whisk for around 10 minutes until the sugar melts into a golden, liquid form, then remove from heat.
2. Add the butter into the pan and slowly whisk the mixture together, ensuring that the butter melts full.
3. Slowly add the whipped cream into the pan whilst still stirring slowly, checking the consistency. This is your homemade caramel sauce – set aside and prep the rest of your dish.
4. On a serving tray, place the cream cheese in the center. Evenly pour the caramel sauce over it – if you have

leftover caramel sauce, you can either serve it in a bowl on the side, or store it in the fridge for up to 2 weeks. Crumble and sprinkle your toffee bits over the top.

5. Serve with sliced apples, pears and pretzels.

2. Italian Inspired Stuffed Mushrooms

Looking for a more filling, warm and hearty appetizer? These Italian-seasoned stuffed mushrooms are a foolproof crowd pleaser! They're bite-sized and oozing with delicious butter, cheese and peppers.

Prep Time: 15 minutes

Cooking Time: 20 minutes

Nutritional Facts/Info:		
36 Servings	Per Serving	
Calories	14	
Carbs	1.5g	1%
Fat	0.8g	1%
Protein	0.5g	

Ingredients:

- 36 portobello whole mushrooms (1 lb)
- ¼ cup chopped onion
- ¼ cup chopped red bell pepper
- 2 tbsp of butter
- 1 ½ cups of breadcrumbs
- 2 tsps of mixed herbs seasoning
- ¼ tsp salt
- ¼ tsp pepper
- ½ tsp chili flakes/powder
- ⅓ cup grated Parmesan cheese

Directions:

1. Preheat the oven to 350°F.
2. Thoroughly wash your mushrooms and twist the stems off to separate them from the mushroom caps.
3. Finely chop your stems and fill ⅓ of a cup with them.
4. In a pan, melt 2 tbsp of butter over medium heat. Toss in the mushroom stems, onions, bell pepper, chilli flakes, salt and pepper and cook for about 3 minutes, stirring regularly. Once the onions have browned and softened, remove from heat and pour in your bread crumbs.
5. Lightly coat an oven tray with 1 tbsp of butter. Fill the mushroom caps with the bread crumb mixture and place them on the oven tray, filled sides facing up.

Sprinkle your Parmesan cheese over the mushroom caps and place in the oven for 15 minutes.

6. Turn your oven function to the Broil option and allow the mushrooms to broil for another minute so that the tops are light brown. Take them out and set them on a platter, serve as hot as possible.

3. Sweet Potato and Cheesy Chorizo Balls

The tie between the savory chorizo and sweet potato flavors are tantalizing to the taste buds, and the aroma alone will have your guests tummies rumbling in excitement to dig in! This is a perfect evening snack before a BBQ or a quick snack during a live sportsmatch over the weekend!

Prep Time: 10 minutes

Cooking Time: 20 minutes

Nutritional Facts/Info:		
8 Servings	Per Serving	
Calories	577	
Carbs	36g	
Fat	36g	
Protein	23g	

Ingredients:

- 1 lb of chorizo sausage
- ½ cup of mashed sweet potato (equal to 1 sweet potato)
- 2 ½ cups of all-purpose baking mix (i.e. Bisquick)
- 1 8-oz pack of shredded Cheddar cheese
- ¼ tsp of cinnamon
- ¼ tsp of salt
- 2 tbsp of orange marmalade
- ¼ cup of pepper sauce
- 1 tsp of Dijon mustard

Directions:

1. Preheat your oven to 350°F and place a baking sheet sprayed with non-stick cooking spray on an oven tray.
2. Mix the chorizo, baking mix, cheese, mashed sweet potato, cinnamon and salt in a bowl until well combined. You can use your hands to massage the spices into the chorizo and sweet potato for a more infused flavor.
3. Break pieces of the mixture into small palm-sized balls, and roll the balls in your palms to smoothen the shape. Place the meatballs evenly apart on the baking tray and place in the oven for 20 minutes.
4. While the meatballs are in the oven, get a small sized bowl out and mix the orange marmalade, pepper sauce and Dijon mustard.

5. Once the meatballs darken in color, remove them from the oven and serve on a platter with the marmalade sauce.

4. Veggie-in-a-Blanket

Inspired by the famous appetizer "pigs-in-a-blanket," this veggie dish is impeccably similar and just as salty, crispy and scrumptious!

Prep Time: 10 minutes

Cooking Time: 15 minutes

Nutritional Facts/Info:		
8 Servings	Per Serving	
Calories	123	
Carbs	3.8g	1%
Fat	7.9g	10%
Protein	8.4g	

Ingredients:

- 4 slices of square cheese (cut diagonally to form triangles)
- 1 pack of veggie cocktail sausages
- 1 can of crescent roll dough
- 1 tbsp of garlic and herb mix
- hot sauce (optional for dip)

Directions:

1. Preheat your oven to 350°F.
2. Cut your dough into triangular shapes (along the perforated lines). Place a slice of triangular cheese and a mini sausage along the widths end of each pastry triangle. Add a drop of garlic and herb mix into each triangle pastry, then roll the pastries around the mini sausages, tucking the leftover pastry at the bottom of each roll.
3. Place the rolls on a baking tray and bake for 14 minutes. Serve while hot.

5. Baba Ghanoush

Baba Ghanoush is a deep rooted staple in Lebanese culture. It's a fantastically healthy appetizer to add to the table, and it's extremely rich and zesty in flavor.

Prep Time: 10 minutes

Cooking Time: 40 minutes

Nutritional Facts/Info:		
4 Servings	Per Serving	
Calories	106	
Carbs	8.7g	3%
Fat	7.8g	10%
Protein	2.5g	

Ingredients:

- 1 eggplant
- 2 tbsps of lemon juice
- 2 tbsps of tahini
- 1 garlic clove (or 1 tsp of garlic paste)
- ½ tsp of salt

- 1 tbsp of olive oil
- a sprinkle of chilli flakes (optional - if you'd like a spicy kick)

Directions:

1. Preheat your oven to 400°F.
2. Wash and poke the eggplant with a fork and place it in the oven for about 35 minutes until tender. Once done, remove from the oven and let it cool.
3. Halve the eggplant and use a spoon to scoop out the flesh. Place the flesh in a blender and add your lemon juice, tahini, garlic, oil, salt and chili flakes. Puree the mixture for about 20 - 30 seconds.
4. Pour the mixture into a bowl/separate smaller bowls and serve with a carb such as Pita bread/chips.

6. Veg Samosas

These bite size Indian delights are the perfect combination of spice, salt and pastry. This recipe is for vegetarian samosas, but you can always substitute the potato for mince, if you'd like a meaty option.

You can also deep fry samosas if you need to save on time!

Prep Time: 20 minutes

Cooking Time: 20 minutes

Nutritional Facts/Info:		
4 Servings	Per Serving	
Calories	153	
Carbs	12.9g	5%
Fat	11.1g	14%
Protein	2g	

Ingredients:

- 1 potato, peeled & cubed
- 2 tbsps of oil
- 1 onion, finely chopped
- ¾ cups of frozen peas & carrots
- 1 tsp of garam masala
- ½ tsp curry powder
- ½ tsp turmeric
- 1 curry leaf
- ½ tsp of mustard seeds
- salt to taste

- 1 sheet of frozen puff pastry (leave it at room temperature for an hour prior to cooking, so it can defrost)

Directions:

1. Preheat the oven to 400°F.
2. Fill a small pot with water and bring to a boil. Add the potatoes into the pot and lower the heat to medium-low. Let it simmer for 15 minutes until potatoes are soft.
3. In a medium pan over medium heat, drizzle a dash of oil in it and add your onions, masala, curry powder, salt, turmeric, curry leaf and mustard seeds. Fry for about 3 minutes until the onions have browned.
4. Incorporate the peas, carrots, peas and potato into the pan with the onions and cook for another 3 minutes, stirring lightly to mix all the spices. You will get a marvelous aroma of spices as you thoroughly mix the contents.
5. Lightly cover an area of your counter with some flour and get a bowl of water ready, with a pastry brush ready.
6. Line an oven tray with parchment paper and keep it aside.
7. Lay your pastry on the flour covered countertop and cut it into 9 equally sized rectangles.

8. Fold over one corner of the rectangle to touch the bottom of the rectangle, creating a cone-like shape. Add a tablespoon of potato filling into the cone shape and then lightly brush the remaining bit of pastry with water. Fold over the remaining pastry around the filling, creating a triangular shape. Repeat for the rest of the samosas.

9. Pop the tray in the oven and bake for 15 minutes.

7. Healthy Crab & Pita Shells

These delicious crab pastries are refreshing and creamy, and will set the perfect mood for a seafood themed lunch/dinner! This recipe requires no cooking time, so if you're pressed for time, this is a quick and yummy bite to make.

Prep Time: 5 minutes

Cooking Time: No Cooking Time

Nutritional Facts/Info:		
6 Servings	Per Serving	
Calories	100	
Carbs	16.2g	6%

Fat	2g	3%
Protein	4.7g	

Ingredients:

- 227g imitation crab meat
- 4 tbsp cream cheese
- 3 tbsp seafood cocktail sauce
- ½ tsp salt
- ½ tsp pepper
- 6 mini pita pockets
- 2 green onions
- Tabasco sauce (for drizzling)

Directions:

1. Dice the crab meat and mix into a bowl with cream cheese, cocktail sauce, salt and pepper.
2. Pour the mixture into the pita pockets.
3. Chop up green onion and garnish the pockets. Drizzle with tabasco sauce and serve.

8. Shrimp Cocktail

Staying on the seafood theme, another creamy and tangy starter option is a shrimp cocktail. The zestiness in the green onion and lemon juice combined with the creaminess from the dressing is a foolproof way to have your guests happy from the moment they walk in!

Prep Time: 10 minutes

Cooking Time: 5 minutes

Nutritional Facts/Info:		
1 Serving	Per Serving	
Calories	196	
Carbs	5.8g	2%
Fat	11.3g	14%
Protein	17.6g	

Ingredients:

- 4 green onions, chopped
- 1 lb cleaned shrimp

- ½ cup Miracle Whip Dressing (alternatively you can mix Mayonnaise and Paprika together).
- a dash of Sriracha/hot sauce
- 20 endive leaves (you can use lettuce/ any sturdy leaf alternative)
- 1 tbsp butter
- ½ tbsp garlic paste
- ½ tsp lemon juice

Directions:

1. Heat up a pan with the butter in it, on medium heat. Once the butter has melted and sizzling, add in your shrimp and garlic paste. Cook for about 5 minutes until the shrimp flesh turns pink.
2. In a separate bowl mix your dressing and lemon juice, and combine the shrimp once cooked and cooled down to room temperature.
3. Wash and separate the endive leaves and plate the leaves facing up - so that they create little bowl-like shapes.
4. Spoon out the shrimp cocktail into the leaves and add a dash of sriracha sauce to each leaf bowl.

9. Caprese Ciabatta

Bread as an appetizer prior to meals is an age-old trick, mostly because it is said to trigger hunger in the body. Something as light as a caprese salad on bread will help prepare your guests for a more filling meal, but also the cheese and tomato is a great neutralizer with not many dominating flavors, so your guests pallets will be prepared for a meal with more powerful flavors and aromas!

Prep Time: 5 minutes

Cooking Time: 10 minutes

Nutritional Facts/Info:		
6 Servings	Per Serving	
Calories	234	
Carbs	17.7g	6%
Fat	12.7g	16%
Protein	11.7g	

Ingredients:

- 1 loaf of ciabatta bread, halved lengthwise

- 4 tbsps of butter
- 2 tbsp garlic paste
- 12 oz. of sliced mozzarella cheese
- ½ cup of balsamic vinegar
- 2 sliced tomatoes
- salt and pepper to taste
- ⅓ cup chopped basil
- rosemary, to taste

Directions:

1. Preheat the oven to 400°F.
2. Layer both halves of the loaf in the oven, with the crust on the bottom, on a baking tray.
3. Mix in your butter, garlic, salt and rosemary in a bowl and evenly spread it over the loaf.
4. Layer the mozzarella slices on the bread - evenly covering the loaf.
5. Pop the loaf in the oven and bake for 15 minutes (until cheese is melted).
6. While the bread is toasting, Pour the balsamic vinegar into a small pan and bring to a boil on the stove. Then lower the heat and let it simmer for about 3 minutes (or until the mixture is halved), then remove from heat and set aside.
7. Once the loaves are done toasting, remove them from the oven and layer some tomato slices on top of the

loaves. Drizzle over the balsamic reduction and garnish with rosemary and basil.

8. Slice the loaves and serve warm.

10. Turkey Meatballs

For a little meatier appetizer, kebabs are always a wonderful choice. These turkey meatballs are a lighter meat option (still high in lean protein) and there are no carbs involved, so it's bite sized and filled with flavor.

Prep Time: 15 minutes

Cooking Time: 10 minutes

Nutritional Facts/Info:		
20 Servings	Per Serving	
Calories	57	
Carbs	2g	1%
Fat	1.9g	2%
Protein	7.8g	

Ingredients:

- 16 oz lean ground turkey breast (1 package)
- ¼ grated/diced red onion
- ½ cup crumbled feta
- 1 tsp oregano
- ½ tsp salt
- ½ garlic powder
- ¼ tsp black pepper
- ¼ tsp dill
- 1 tbsp olive oil

Directions:

1. Preheat the oven to broil on 400°F and place the oven rack about 5 inches from the broiler.
2. Lightly drizzle oil on an oven tray and set aside.
3. In a bowl, combine all the ingredients and spices. It's best to use your hands so that you can massage the spice into the meat.
4. Scoop out the meat mixture and roll them into palm sized meatballs (about 20), and place on the oven tray.
5. Place the meatballs in the oven for 8-10 minutes until they're a light brown in color. Serve with toothpicks & while hot.

Chapter 3: Pasta

Originating in Italy, this gloriously versatile dough can be worked into so many different meals, combining itself with almost any ingredient and enhancing all the flavors and aromas perfectly – and the best part is that pasta can be both time and money efficient! From pasta salads for lunch to bolognese for dinner, from penne to fettuccine, ravioli to macaroni – these ten recipes will help you understand how to prep different pastas, and which types of pastas will bring out the best flavor and texture when combined with certain ingredients and dishes!

1. Spaghetti Napolitana

Spaghetti Napolitana is a basic recipe of a flat/long style of pasta mixed with a tangy tomato chutney. It is the base to adding many more ingredients or can be a meal on its own! This Napolitana recipe requires only the basic ingredients and is quick to make, yet still maintains a warm and homey feel through the aromas and taste.

Prep Time: 5 minutes

Cooking Time: 15 minutes

Nutritional Facts/Info:		
4 Servings	Per Serving	
Calories	517	
Carbs	79g	29%
Fat	15.9g	20%
Protein	16.3g	

Ingredients:

- 500g dried spaghetti
- ¼ cup of olive oil
- 1 tbsp of crushed garlic
- 1 onion
- a pinch of salt and pepper
- ½ tsp chilli powder (optional)
- 2 curry leaves (optional)
- 800g of chopped tomato
- ¼ cup of basil
- 200g Parmesan cheese (shredded)

Directions:

1. Bring a large pot filled halfway with water and a pinch of salt, to boil. Add in your spaghetti and leave to cook for about 8-10 minutes.

2. While the pasta cooks, prepare your Napolitana sauce – heat a pan with a drizzle of oil in it, over medium heat. Add your garlic, onions, salt, pepper, chili powder and curry leaves into the pan and cook until the onions have browned. Then pour in your tomatoes and ½ a cup of water and leave to simmer for 5 minutes.

3. Once your spaghetti is cooked, use a colander to drain your pasta and plate it. Pour in your Napolitana sauce, and sprinkle the basil and Parmesan on top.

2. Mushroom & Spinach Shells

This wholesome and hearty meal offers a fantastic way of how to prepare and serve shell shaped pasta – which is best served with chutney/sauce that can fill up within the pasta shells. Therefore each individual bite is an experience on its own!

Prep Time: 25 minutes

Cooking Time: 40 minutes

Nutritional Facts/Info:		
4 Servings	Per Serving	
Calories	519	
Carbs	62.7g	23%
Fat	17.6g	23%
Protein	28.4g	

Ingredients:

- 6 oz of jumbo pasta shells (20 shells)
- 3 tsp of salt, divided
- ¾ tsp black pepper
- 1 chopped yellow onion
- 3 tbsp of garlic paste
- 1 28-oz can of crushed tomatoes
- 8 oz of mixed sliced wild mushrooms
- 5 cups of chopped baby spinach
- 1 16-oz container of whole-milk ricotta cheese
- 1 cup of grated Parmesan cheese

Directions:

1. Preheat the oven to 400°F.

2. Fill a medium pot halfway with water and add a pinch of salt. Place over medium-high heat and bring to a boil. Pour in your pasta shells and lower heat to medium-low. Cook until al-dente – about 7-10 minutes (the pasta shells shouldn't be too soft as they need to also cook in the oven).

3. While the pasta boils, place 1 tbsp of oil in a separate skillet over medium heat. Add in your onion and garlic and fry until the onions have browned. Add the tomatoes, 1 ½ tsp of salt and ½ tsp of pepper into the skillet and slowly stir for about 5 minutes until the sauce starts to thicken.

4. Check on your pasta and drain the shells, using a colander. Set the shells aside to cool down.

5. In another skillet, pour 1 tbsp of oil and bring it to a medium heat. Add in the mushrooms, ¼ tsp salt, ½ tsp pepper and cook for about 5 minutes until the mushrooms have browned. Then add in your spinach and cook for another minute until the spinach is slightly wilted.

6. In a baking tray, lightly layer the tray with a drizzle of oil and pour the tomato sauce in – reserve ½ a cup of the sauce for later.

7. Fill the pasta shells with ricotta, mushrooms and spinach and layer the shells over the tomato sauce, in the baking tray.

8. Pour the remainder ½ cup of tomato over the shells and sprinkle Parmesan cheese over.

9. Bake for 15 minutes.

3. Eggplant & Olive Pasta Salad

For a lighter lunch/dinner addition – pasta salads are a wonderful option! They're great to pack for lunch, they stay fresh all day long and won't make you too lethargic but will definitely fill you up! Pasta salads are also great as an addition to the dinner table if you need some extra carbs in the meal, or have some ingredients that you'd like to throw together as a side dish. The eggplant and olive pasta will give you a lovely vinegary kick that will wake your taste buds up and give you a good boost of energy. It's a great option for how to make use of short pasta, such as fusilli, because they help keep the bite-sizes small, yet filling!

Prep Time: 10 minutes

Cooking Time: 20 minutes

Nutritional Facts/Info:		
4 Servings	Per Serving	
Calories	521	

Carbs	54g	
Fat	30g	
Protein	11g	

Ingredients:

- 6 oz of short pasta (such as fusilli/farfalle)
- 1 eggplant (chopped into ¾ inch squares)
- 6 divided tbsp of olive oil
- 2 tbsp red wine vinegar
- 1 tsp salt
- ¼ tsp black pepper
- 1 tbsp chopped oregano
- 2 oz of crumbled feta cheese
- 1 ½ cups of cherry tomatoes, halved
- 1 cup of pitted olives

Directions:

1. Set your oven to preheat at 475ºF.
2. On a baking tray, lay out the chopped eggplant and olives, and drizzle with 3 tbsp of olive oil. Pop it in the oven and roast for 20 minutes until the eggplant has softened.
3. While the eggplant and olives are roasting, fill a pot halfway with water and a pinch of salt and set the heat

to a medium – bringing the water to a boil. Then toss in your pasta and lower the heat to medium-low. Let the pasta simmer for about 10 minutes.

4. In a separate bowl, whisk the vinegar, salt, pepper, oregano and 3 tbsp of oil together.

5. Once the pasta has softened, drain it through a colander. Remove the roast vegetables from the oven, once cooked.

6. Mix the pasta, vegetables, crumbled feta and vinegar mixture in a bowl and garnish with oregano.

4. Greens Pasta Salad

Keeping to the theme of pasta salads, another fun and zesty salad idea is to mix in some crunchy greens, lemon juice and chili. These types of crunchy pasta salads make the best summertime lunches as they're extremely healthy, filling and give you that added energy boost to continue with your day! A pasta that will work well with these salads are short, twisted pastas such as gemelli or orecchiette – these are perfect for small, bite-sizes and trap a lot of juice and seasoning in their hollows of the pasta's shape.

Prep Time: 15 minutes

Cooking Time: 25 minutes

Nutritional Facts/Info:		
12 Servings	Per Serving	
Calories	262	
Carbs	31g	
Fat	11g	
Protein	8g	

Ingredients:

- 1 lb of short pasta
- 1 lb of sliced cucumber
- 8 oz of crumbled feta cheese
- 1 tsp of salt
- 6 tbsp olive oil
- 2 tbsp of mustard
- 1 tsp of lemon zest
- 6 tbsps of lemon juice
- 2 cloves of garlic, grated
- ½ tsp of black pepper
- ½ tsp of crushed chilli
- 1 pack of cilantro leaves
- ½ cup of mint

Directions:

1. Fill a medium-sized pot halfway with water and add a pinch of salt. Bring the water to boil then add in your pasta. Cook for 10 minutes until al dente, then drain the pasta using a colander.
2. Place the pasta into a large/wide bowl and add 2 tbsps of oil. Toss until the pasta is evenly coated.
3. In a separate bowl, whisk mustard, lemon zest, lemon juice, garlic, salt, pepper, 4 tbsp of oil and crushed chilli together. Add in the cucumbers and feta to the bowl and toss/gently stir with a big spoon until all the contents are well mixed.
4. Combine the pasta and the mix together and give it one last mix. Garnish your pasta salad with cilantro and mint just before serving and you have the perfect summer pasta salad!

5. Chicken & Chickpea Pasta Soup

On a more colder, wintery day, pasta can also be added into your soup to incorporate the carb element into the meal! *Orecchiette* pasta translated from Italian, means "little ears", given their tiny, rounded shape. Similar pasta options that you can add to your soup are shorter pastas such as bow tie pasta (known as farfalle) or penne.

Prep Time: 20 minutes

Cooking Time: 35 minutes

Nutritional Facts/Info:		
4 Servings	Per Serving	
Calories	909	
Carbs	98.3g	36%
Fat	40g	51%
Protein	45.2g	

Ingredients:

- 1 cup of thinly sliced leeks
- 1 cup of chopped carrots
- 6 cups of chicken broth
- 8 tbsps of olive oil, divided
- 1¾ tsps of salt, divided
- ¾ tsps of black pepper, divided
- ½ cup of grated Parmesan cheese
- 1 cup of orecchiette pasta
- 2 cups of shredded chicken
- 1 tbsp of garlic paste
- 1 15-oz. can chickpeas, drained and rinsed

- 2 tablespoons lemon juice, divided
- ¼ cup of roasted almonds
- 1 cup basil leaves
- ½ cup of parsley

Directions:

1. Drizzle a tbsp of oil into a large saucepan over medium-high heat. Once the oil is sizzling, place in your shredded chicken, garlic paste and a tsp of salt. Fry for about 10 minutes.

2. Once cooked, place the chicken in a separate bowl, then combine the leeks and carrots into the pot and stir for about 5 minutes.

3. Mix in the broth, 1 tsp salt and ½ a tsp of pepper and bring to a boil. Reduce the heat to medium-low, cover the pan and leave to simmer for about 12 minutes.

4. While the vegetables cook, bring another pot to boil, filled halfway with water and a pinch of salt. Pour in your pasta and leave to boil for 10 minutes.

5. Drain the pasta through a colander and mix the pasta into the vegetable pot. Add in the chicken and chickpeas and stir for 5 minutes.

6. Whilst the contents in the pot are slow-cooking on a medium-low heat, mix the almonds, basil, parsley, lemon juice, 7 tbsps of oil, ¾ tbsp of salt and ¼ tsp of pepper into a food processor and process until it is a

smooth liquid. Transfer the mix into a small bowl and mix in the parmesan cheese.

7. Remove your soup from the heat and serve in a bowl, topped with the parmesan mix.

6. Spaghetti Bolognese

Spaghetti Bolognese is definitely one of the more popular Italian dishes, especially from the pasta category. It's a simple, yet divine combination of beef and tomato paste that has consistently proven to be a successful meal option!

Prep Time: 15 minutes

Cooking Time: 1 hour 30 minutes

Nutritional Facts/Info:		
4 Servings	Per Serving	
Calories	136	
Carbs	12.9g	5%
Fat	4.1g	5%
Protein	13.7g	

Ingredients:

- ¼ lb Italian sausage, sliced
- 3 oz of ground beef
- 2 ½ tbsp minced onion
- ½ tsp crushed garlic
- ¼ can of crushed tomatoes
- ½ can of tomato paste
- ½ can of tomato sauce
- 1 ½ tsps sugar
- ½ tsp dried basil
- ⅛ tsp fennel seeds
- ¼ tsp mixed herb seasoning
- ½ tsp salt
- ½ tsp pepper
- 1 tbsp oil
- ½ cup of spaghetti

Directions:

1. Heat the oil in a medium pot over medium heat. Pour in your onions, seasoning, salt, pepper, basil, fennel and sugar and let it simmer for 1 minute. Add in the sausage, beef and garlic and cook for 10 minutes.

2. Drain out the excess fat from the pot, then add in your tomato paste, tomato sauce, crushed tomatoes and 2 tbsps of water. Lower the heat to the lowest level and cover the pot, leaving it to simmer for 1 ½ hours.

3. While the bolognese cooks, fill a medium sized pot halfway with water and a pinch of salt. Bring the pot to boil and add in the spaghetti. Lower the heat to medium-high and boil for 12-15 minutes. Drain the pasta using a colander and set aside.

4. Once the bolognese is ready, combine the pasta with the sauce and serve.

7. Zuppa Toscana Gnocchi Soup

Famously known as one of Olive Garden's specialties, Gnocchi Zuppa Toscana soup is a creamy divine wonder of Gnocchi, bacon and Italian sausage in a warm and delightful soup.

Prep Time: 10 minutes

Cooking Time: 20 minutes

Nutritional Facts/Info:		
6 Servings	Per Serving	
Calories	437	
Carbs	26g	9%
Fat	30g	46%
Protein	16g	32%

Ingredients:

- 1 lb potato gnocchi
- 4 slices of bacon, diced
- 1 lb of Italian sausage
- 6 cups of chicken broth
- 1 tbsp of olive oil
- 1 diced yellow onion
- 4 tbsps of garlic paste
- 2 cups of chopped kale
- ½ cup of heavy cream
- grated parmesan cheese for serving

Directions:

1. Boil the gnocchi in a pot filled halfway with water for about 10 minutes. Drain the pasta using a colander and set the gnocchi aside.
2. Drizzle olive oil into a medium-large pot and bring to a medium-high heat. Add in your diced bacon, garlic and onions and fry for 2 minutes. Then throw in the Italian sausage and break it apart using a wooden spoon. Cook for about 5 minutes until the sausage meat is thoroughly cooked.
3. Mix in the chicken broth, salt, pepper and reduce the heat to a medium-low. Mix in the gnocchi and kale and cook for another 5 minutes.
4. Pour in the heavy cream and stir slowly for 2 minutes.

5. Remove from heat and serve in bowls with parmesan sprinkled on top.

8. Cheesy Ravioli and Italian Sausage

Another delicious, meaty and cheesy dish perfect for a main dinner meal is this outstanding cheesy ravioli and Italian sausage dish. Ravioli are pastry pockets filled with different ingredients – this specific recipe calls for cheesy ravioli.

Prep Time: 15 minutes

Cooking Time: 10 minutes

Nutritional Facts/Info:		
4 Servings	Per Serving	
Calories	699	
Carbs	36.4g	13%
Fat	45.3g	58%
Protein	36.1g	

Ingredients:

- 1 tbsp of olive oil

- 1 lb Italian sausage
- 1 can of diced tomatoes
- 1 can of tomato sauce
- 1 tbsp of tomato paste
- 1 ½ tsp Italian seasoning
- 1 tsp of garlic paste
- ¼ onion, diced
- 16 oz (1 packet) of cheese ravioli
- 1 cup shredded mozzarella cheese
- ½ cup grated parmesan cheese
- 5 basil leaves, chopped
- 1 tsp salt
- ½ tsp black pepper

Directions:

1. Prepare your ravioli by boiling it in half a pot of water and a pinch of salt for 10 minutes, then strain the water out by using a colander. Set aside.

2. Drizzle the olive oil into a skillet and bring to a medium heat. Mix in the Italian sausage, onions and garlic paste and fry for about 5 minutes, crumbling the sausage as it cooks.

3. Pour in the tomatoes, tomato sauce, tomato paste and Italian seasoning and stir. Then add in your ravioli and 1 ¼ cups of water and bring the mix to a boil. Cover the

pot and reduce the heat and leave to simmer for about 10 minutes.

4. Preheat your oven to 350°F and set to broiler.
5. Remove from heat once the ravioli is soft. Transfer the contents of the skillet into an oven safe pan, sprinkle the pasta with mozzarella and parmesan. Place in the oven for 4 minutes so that the cheese melts well over the pasta.
6. Garnish with basil and serve hot!

9. Shrimp Gnocchi

Shrimp, pasta and creamy butter sounds like a perfect, heartily meal for something that can be prepared in 30 minutes!

Prep Time: 10 minutes

Cooking Time: 20 minutes

Nutritional Facts/Info:		
4 Servings	Per Serving	
Calories	511	
Carbs	38.7g	14%

Fat	31.5g	40%
Protein	20.8g	

Ingredients:

- 1 pack potato gnocchi
- 8 oz of shrimp (cleaned, peeled and deveined)
- 8 tbsp butter
- 2 tbsp garlic paste
- 2 tbsp olive oil
- ⅓ cup chicken stock
- lemon juice (to drizzle)

Directions:

1. Bring a pot of water to boil and add the gnocchi in. Boil for about 10 minutes then drain the pasta using a colander.
2. In a medium sized pan, drizzle a little olive oil and bring to a medium heat. Add the gnocchi into the pan and cook for about 2 minutes, then flip them over and cook the other side – it should turn a nice golden brown.
3. Remove the gnocchi, then add 2 tbsps of butter into the pan, then throw in the shrimp, salt and pepper. Fry for about 2 minutes on either side, until the shrimp turns a reddish-pink in color.

4. Remove the shrimp and then add your garlic, chicken stock and lemon juice. Raise the heat and bring to a boil, then lower the heat to a simmer, slowly adding in your 6 tbsps of butter, allowing it to slowly melt.
5. Combine the gnocchi and shrimp back into the pan and toss to mix the flavors together. Serve while hot.

10. Beef Lasagna

Lasagna is a meal that can definitely go a long way. It's an extremely time efficient meal to prepare for the week while also being extremely cheesy, meaty and filling!

Prep Time: 15 minutes

Cooking Time: 1 hour

Nutritional Facts/Info:		
8 Servings	Per Serving	
Calories	414	
Carbs	36.1g	13%
Fat	14g	18%
Protein	36.2g	

Ingredients:

- 1 tbsp olive oil
- 1 lb of ground beef
- ½ an onion, diced
- ¾ cup bell pepper, diced
- 2 tbsp garlic paste
- 1 can of tomato sauce
- 3 oz of tomato paste
- 1 can of crushed tomato
- 2 tbsp of crushed oregano
- ¼ cup chopped parsley
- 1 tbsp of Italian seasoning
- 1 tbsp of white wine vinegar
- 1 tbsp sugar
- ½ tbsp salt
- ½ lb dry lasagna noodles (alternatively any flat, long pasta)
- 15 oz of Ricotta cheese
- 24 oz of mozzarella cheese, grated
- 4 oz of grated parmesan cheese

Directions:

1. In a large pot, fill ¾ of water and add a pinch of salt. Bring the pot to boil and add in your pasta. Let it boil for about 12-15 minutes (or until soft).

2. While the pasta boils, take a large pan and drizzle 2 tsp of oil into it and set to medium-high heat. Add in your ground beef, garlic and onions and fry until the meat is brown. Use a slotted spoon to separate the meat from the fat and set the meat in a separate bowl on the side.

3. Add in the bell peppers and cook for about 2 minutes until they're softened, then add the meat back to the pan and leave on a low heat.

4. Remove your pasta from the pot and drain it using a colander. Set aside to cool down.

5. Transfer the contents from the pan into a medium sized pot, adding the tomatoes, tomato sauce and tomato paste. Leave the pot on a medium heat. Throw in your Italian seasoning, parsley, oregano, salt and white wine vinegar. Stir well and then add in sugar.

6. Bring the sauce to a low simmer and leave to cook for about 20 minutes.

7. While the sauce cooks, preheat your oven to 375°F and get a baking tray out. Coat the bottom with a little oil and lay your pasta sheets in the oil (try to evenly coat the pasta in oil so that it doesn't stick together.

8. Next, get a casserole dish out and start the layering process. Place the noodles along the bottom and then scoop out some of the sauce to evenly coat the pasta in the dish. Next, sprinkle some parmesan and mozzarella

over the sauce. Repeat the layers until you finish your ingredients.

9. Cover the casserole dish with foil and bake in the oven for 45 minutes. You can remove the foil and bake for an extra 10 minutes if you'd like a more crusty top layer.

10. The lasagna is ready to serve! You can store the rest in the refrigerator for up to 5 days.

Chapter 4: Pizza

From deep dish, cheesy, thick crusted, Chicago pizzas to Mexican slices, Hawaiian, pan pizza, focaccia and thin crust New York slices – pizza has marked a long-lasting place in everyone's heart. Another fantastic dish that originated in Italy, pizza was first formed as thin crusted flatbread, drizzled in garlic and olive oil – years later, it has now transformed into a glorious diverse meal category of its own.

1. The Best Homemade Pizza Dough with Basic Tomato Base

Mastering the art of making a good pizza dough is the true secret to any delicious pizza! The ingredients and toppings are only half of what makes pizza truly delicious, so here is a simple recipe to make your own homemade pizza dough and a simple tomato base.

Prep Time: 1 hour 30 minutes (1 hour is used to allow the dough to sit at room temperature)

Cooking Time: 15 minutes

Nutritional Facts/Info:		
4 Servings (2 pizzas)	Per Serving	
Calories	920	
Carbs	188.4g	69%
Fat	7g	9%
Protein	28.4g	

Ingredients:

For the dough:

- 3 ½ cups of all-purpose flour (plus another cup for your hands and coating the surface)
- 1 ⅓ cups of warm water
- 2 ¼ tsp of instant yeast
- 2 tbsp olive oil
- 1 tbsp sugar
- ¾ tsp salt

For the tomato base:

- 6 oz of tomato paste
- 15 oz of tomato sauce

- 2 tbsp of oregano
- 2 tbsp of Italian seasoning
- ½ tsp garlic powder
- ½ tsp onion powder
- ½ tsp garlic salt
- ¼ ground black pepper
- 1 tsp sugar
- 200 g of mozzarella (optional)

Directions:

1. In a medium sized bowl, whisk together the water, yeast and sugar. Next, slowly pour in the olive oil, salt and flour, while whisking carefully.

2. Lightly cover a working space with flour and place your dough mixture onto it. Using your hands, knead the dough for about 4 minutes, it should start to feel soft and stretchy. Poke your dough with your finger – if the dough boz back, it is ready to rise; if not, continue kneading for another minute or so.

3. Grease the medium sized bowl with a dash of oil and place the dough into the boil. Turn it over, so that all sides of the dough are well-coated in oil. Cover the bowl with a towel or foil and set it aside for about an hour, allowing the dough to rise at room temperature.

4. While the dough is rising, you can prep the tomato base: In a medium bowl, combine your tomato paste and sauce and mix well, until there are no more lumps.

5. If you are using mozzarella/any cheese, grate it finely and add into the bowl.

6. Mix the rest of your ingredients into the bowl: oregano, Italian seasoning, garlic powder, onion powder, garlic salt, pepper and sugar. Cover the bowl and set aside.

7. Once the hour is almost up, preheat your oven to 475°F and lightly grease a baking tray with oil.

8. When the dough has risen, punch into the center of it so that all the air bubbles are released and divide the dough in half. On a lightly floured working space, use a rolling pin to roll the dough halves into two circular shapes.

9. Place the two circular doughs onto your baking tray and, using your hands, lift a small piece of the edge up, so to create a crust around the circumference (this will help you when you add filling to the center of the pizza).

10. Place in the oven for about 10 minutes until the pizza starts to brown up. Remove the pizzas and layer them with the tomato base mixture.

11. Pop the pizzas back in the oven for another 5-10 minutes (depending on the ingredients – e.g. cheese may take longer to melt).

12. Serve hot and you can always freeze the extra pizza for up to 3 months, and reheat in the oven when you feel for it!

2. Deep Dish Pizza

Best known in Chicago, deep dishes are mouth-wateringly delicious and filled with flavors, all tied together with cheese and tomato sauce mixes. It's sort of similar to a pie, but without the pastry topping: More filling, more cheese!

Prep Time: 90 minutes

Cooking Time: 20 minutes

Nutritional Facts/Info:		
8 Servings	Per Serving	
Calories	185	
Carbs	28.2g	10%
Fat	5.4g	7%
Protein	5.8g	

Ingredients:

For the dough:

- ¾ cup of warm water
- 1 tbsp sugar
- 2 ¼ tsp of instant yeast
- 2 cups of all-purpose flour
- 1 ½ tsp salt
- 2 tbsp olive oil

For the topping:

- 2 tbsp cornmeal
- cooking spray/oil to drizzle
- 2 cups of shredded mozzarella
- 32 oz of marinara (this can be substituted for the tomato base recipe in no. 1)
- 1 tsp of Italian seasoning
- ½ tsp of garlic paste
- ¼ cup of grated parmesan
- (if you'd like to mix in any minced meat or extra toppings, prep them while the dough is rising at room temp.)

Directions:

1. Refer to recipe no. 1 to make the dough, and leave the dough to rise for 90 minutes while you prepare the rest!

2. Once 90 minutes is almost up and the dough has risen, preheat your oven to 450°F and get an oven safe skillet/deep pan. Grease the pan with cooking spray or a drizzle of oil.

3. Sprinkle some flour on a working surface and lay your dough on the surface. Using a rolling pin, roll the dough into a circular shape – about 12 inches in diameter, or according to the pan's circumference (remember that this dough will need to cover the base and the sides of the pan).

4. Place the dough onto the base of the pan and press the remaining dough around the sides of the pan.

5. In a small bowl, stir in the marinara sauce, garlic pasta and Italian seasoning. Pour the mixture into the pan and then sprinkle the mozzarella and parmesan cheese over the top.

6. Bake for 20 minutes, checking that the crust is a golden brown.

3. New York Slice

Famously known for its thin crust and large sliced servings, New York-style pizza is best for when you're craving that fine balance between topping to crust ratio.

Prep Time: 24 hours – This recipe requires prep for the dough at least one day before cooking, so that the dough is given time to rest – be sure to prepare in advance/use recipe no. 1 for a quicker dough alternative.

Cooking Time: 30 minutes

Nutritional Facts/Info:		
8 Servings (3 pizzas)	Per Serving	
Calories	387	
Carbs	64g	23%
Fat	8.6g	11%
Protein	12.6g	

Ingredients:

- 4 ½ cups of all-purpose flour

- 1 ½ tbsp of sugar
- 3 tsp of salt
- 2 tsp of instant yeast
- 3 tbsp of olive oil
- 1 batch of NY Style sauce (alternatively you can make the homemade version – attached below)
- 15 oz of warm water
- 4 cups of grated mozzarella cheese
- 1 cup of fresh basil leaves

For NY Style Sauce:

- 1 can of tomato puree
- 1 tbsp of olive oil
- 1 tbsp of butter
- 2 tbsp garlic paste
- 1 tsp of oregano
- a dash of chilli flakes
- 1 ½ tsp salt, to taste
- half a yellow onion, sliced thinly
- 1 tsp of sugar

Directions:

Preparation the day before:

1. For the dough: In a food processor (alternatively you can mix by hand), combine your flour, 1 ½ tsp sugar, 3 tsp salt and yeast and pulse until mixed. Pour in the 3

tbsp of oil and water and mix until the dough starts to form (about 20-30 seconds).

2. Lightly flour a working space, place the dough on the space and knead it by hand until the dough is smooth. Divide the dough into 3 even parts and place in zip-lock bags for at least one day.

The next day:

1. Remove the dough from the freezer 2 hours prior, shape the dough parts into balls and place in a bowl covered with plastic wrap, allowing the dough to rise at room temperature.

2. While the dough rises, prepare the NY Sauce (if you have the sauce, skip this step). Melt butter in a pan over medium-low heat. Drop the garlic, oregano, chilli flakes and salt into the pan and stir for about 3 minutes, until you can smell the aromas of the spices.

3. Pour in the tomato puree, halved onions and sugar. Bring the heat up to a simmer and then to the lowest setting. Leave to simmer for about 30 minutes and then season with salt to taste. Set the mix aside.

4. 1 hour prior to baking, preheat the oven to 500°F. Roll your dough balls out into circular shapes (about 12 inch circles), fold the outer inches of the dough inwards, so that it forms the crusty circumference.

5. Transfer the pizza doughs onto a rack, or lightly cover a baking tray with a drizzle of oil and place the pizza doughs on that.

6. Pour the sauce and sprinkle the cheeses evenly over the pizzas (and add any additional toppings of your choice) and bake for 15 minutes until golden brown. Sprinkle basil leaves and olive oil over the top, once baked and serve hot.

4. Primavera Skillet Pizza

Primavera is well known and differentiated from other pizzas/pastas because it mainly consists of sautéed vegetables layered on a thin, crisp pizza base.

Prep Time: 15 minutes

Cooking Time: 45 minutes

Nutritional Facts/Info:		
2 Servings	Per Serving	
Calories	553	
Carbs	73g	27%
Fat	17.1g	22%
Protein	27.4g	

Ingredients:

- 1 lb of pizza dough at room temp (refer to recipe no.1 for homemade pizza dough)
- 2 bell peppers, sliced lengthwise
- ½ a head of broccoli, washed and florets separated
- ¼ red onion, thinly sliced
- 1 cup of cherry tomatoes
- 2 tbsp of olive oil
- salt to taste
- pepper to taste
- 1 tsp of crushed chilli
- all-purpose flour (for dusting the working surface)
- 1 cup of ricotta cheese
- 1 cup of shredded mozzarella

Directions:

1. Preheat the oven to 400°F. Wash and cut the vegetables. Place them on a baking tray and drizzle with olive oil, salt and pepper.
2. Roast the vegetables for about 20 minutes, then remove and raise the oven temperature to 500°F.
3. Flour your working surface and roll the dough out into a flat, circular form – about 12 inches in diameter.
4. Drizzle a baking tray with olive oil and place the pizza base on the tray.
5. Cut the cherry tomatoes into halves.

6. Layer spoonfuls of ricotta on the dough and then evenly sprinkle mozzarella over it. Layer the roast vegetables on top and drizzle with olive oil, then sprinkle salt, pepper and chilli flakes to taste.
7. Bake for 12 minutes until the cheese melts.

5. Pan-Fried Pizza

The 1960's bred the glorious franchise known as Pizza-Hut, where the company developed the delicious mixture of cheese, pan-fried (yet not greasy) base–which is an experience on its own, from its crusted outer surface to the soft, moist inner piece.

Prep Time: 1 hour

Cooking Time: 20 minutes

Nutritional Facts/Info:		
6 Pizzas	Per Serving	
Calories	305	
Carbs	26.1g	9%
Fat	13g	17%
Protein	21g	42%

Ingredients:

- 1 pack of pizza dough (or refer to recipe no.1 for a homemade pizza dough recipe)
- 4 tbsp of oil for frying
- 1 cup of tomato paste (or refer to recipe no.1 for a homemade version)
- ½ cup of shredded mozzarella (you can always add more for extra cheesiness)
- 4 tbsp of pesto
- a handful of fresh basil
- ¼ cup of parmesan cheese
- ¼ cup of feta cheese (optional)
- a dash of sweet chilli sauce

Directions:

1. Prepare the homemade dough/the premade pizza dough and allow sufficient time for it to rise at room temperature.
2. Once the dough has risen, divide it into 6 equal parts and flatten, then roll the bases out into circular shapes (6 inches in diameter). Try not to roll it too thin as it needs to fry, so ensure about ½ an inch in thickness.
3. In a large frying pan, heat up the oil on a medium-low heat.

4. Fry the pizza bases for 30 seconds on either side, until golden brown and transfer to a paper towel, to drain the excess oil.

5. Preheat the oven to 450°F and take a baking tray out. Line the fried pizza bases on the tray and layer the tomato paste, a dash of sweet chilli sauce and the cheeses evenly on each pizza. Bake for 5-10 minutes until the cheese has melted and is crisp.

6. Garnish with basil and pesto and serve warm.

6. Cauliflower Crust Pizza

Cauliflower is such a diverse ingredient that can be brought into any meal and/or substitute an ingredient that you may not have, or the substitution may just be for a healthier alternative! Not to mention, it's also much quicker to make!

Prep Time: 15 minutes

Cooking Time: 30 minutes

Nutritional Facts/Info:		
2 Servings	Per Serving	
Calories	130	

Carbs	8.2g	3%
Fat	6.5g	8%
Protein	11.4g	

Ingredients:

- 1 head of cauliflower
- 2 eggs
- 1 cup of shredded mozzarella (divided in half)
- ¼ cup of grated parmesan
- ½ tsp of dried oregano
- ½ tsp of salt
- ¼ tsp of garlic powder
- 1 can of tomato paste
- a handful of basil leaves
- 1 tsp of chili

Directions:

1. Line a baking tray with parchment paper and set aside. Preheat the oven to 400°F.
2. Break the cauliflower into tiny florets and either pulse in a food processor/blend until fine.
3. Steam the cauliflower in a steam bowl. Alternatively, you can place the cauliflower in a sieve over a pot with boiling water, cover the lid, and allow it to steam for

about 5 minutes. Drain the cauliflower and leave it out on a paper towel to dry.

4. Beat the eggs with a fork, then mix in the cauliflower, mozzarella, parmesan, oregano, salt and garlic powder. Pour the mixture out into the center of the baking sheet, creating the form and size of a pizza base and bake for 20 minutes.

5. While the pizza bakes, mix the can of tomato paste with the chili.

6. Remove the pizza from the oven after 20 minutes (it should look a little golden brown), and pour the tomato paste over the base. Sprinkle the remaining mozzarella and place back in the oven for an additional 10 minutes.

7. Top the pizza off with some basil leaves and serve hot.

7. St. Louis Style Pizza

The St. Louis pizza title pays homage to its hometown: St. Louis. It's specifically recognized for its thin crust and thin layered toppings. The special factors in the recipe that makes this style of pizza distinct from the rest, is that there is no yeast in the dough and there is the prominent use of Provel cheese. The pizza slices are also cut into squares/rectangles.

Prep Time: 30 minutes

Cooking Time: 20 minutes

Nutritional Facts/Info:		
Per Slice of Pizza (8 Slices on medium pizza)	Per Serving	
Calories	168	
Carbs	19g	6%
Fat	6g	9%
Protein	8g	16%

Ingredients:

- 2 ¼ cups of all-purpose flour
- 1 tsp of baking powder
- 2 tsp of olive oil
- 2 tsp of corn syrup
- ¾ cup of warm water
- 10 oz of crushed tomato
- 3 oz of tomato paste
- 1 tsp of sugar
- 1 tsp of basil seasoning
- ½ tsp of oregano

- 1 tsp garlic powder
- 1 ½ tsp of salt, divided
- 4 cups of shredded provel cheese

Directions:

1. Preheat the oven to 550°F and place a pizza stone in the oven, if you have one.
2. Whisk the flour, ½ tsp of salt and baking powder together and then slowly pour in the water, oil and corn syrup whilst slowly whisking. Mix and knead the dough until smooth and all the ingredients are mixed in.
3. Lightly flour a working surface and divide the dough into 2 equal halves, then roll each half into a circular shape – about 12 inches in diameter.
4. In a separate bowl, whisk together your tomato puree, tomato paste, sugar, remaining 1 tsp of salt, garlic powder and oregano.
5. Pour the sauce over the pizzas, coating them well. Sprinkle Provel cheese over the tops and add basil, oregano and salt seasoning to top it off. Place the pizzas on a baking tray/pizza stone for 10 minutes, ensuring that the cheese has fully melted and golden brown.
6. Cut the pizza into square/rectangular slices and you have yourself a St. Louis pizza!

8. Detroit-Style Pepperoni Pizza

Pepperoni originally started as cured, spicy sausage in butcheries in lower Italy, but was brought over to New York in the 1920s. Thus, the craze for pepperoni pizzas was sparked.

Detroit-style pizzas are thick crusted and square shaped, somewhat similar to a pan pizza in texture.

Prep Time: 90 minutes (for dough to rise)

Cooking Time: 20 minutes

Nutritional Facts/Info:		
8 Servings	Per Serving	
Calories	560	
Carbs	35.8g	13%
Fat	35.1g	45%
Protein	24.9g	

Ingredients:

-   4 tbsps of olive oil, divided

- 1 batch of pizza dough (use recipe no. 1 of this chapter for homemade dough)
- 8 oz of sliced pepperoni
- 16 oz of mozzarella cheese, cut into ½ inch cubes
- 2 tsp of Italian seasoning
- 2 tbsps of garlic paste
- 1 can of crushed tomatoes
- 2 tsps of sugar
- salt and pepper to taste

Directions:

1. Prepare the dough through recipe no. 1 of this chapter, or take the store-bought dough out and leave to rise at room temperature for at least 1 hour.

2. While the dough is rising, prepare the sauce: using a small pan, drizzle some oil to lightly coat the surface and bring to a medium heat. Sprinkle in the Italian seasoning and garlic paste and mix the aromas until fragrant. Pour the tomatoes into the pot and add the sugar, salt and pepper to taste. Lower the heat and allow the mix to simmer for about 30 minutes. Set aside to cool.

3. Once the dough is almost ready and the sauce has cooled, preheat the oven to 550°F. Get a large, square pan and drizzle oil to coat the base. Place the dough in

the pan and press it down, to evenly fill the base of the pan.

4. Layer the sauce over the pizza base, then evenly place slices of pepperoni and cheese cubes over the sauce.

5. Bake for about 15 minutes, until the cheese has melted and golden brown. Once the pizza is ready, cut it into square slices and serve.

Are you enjoying this book? If so, I'd like to hear your thoughts: please leave a short review on Amazon. Thank you.

Chapter 5: Chicken

For all the poultry lovers, the recipes in this chapter will cover the perfect chicken dishes for any occasion – from themed dinner parties, to barbecues, to a cold wintery evening, we've included our top ten meals for every occasion! If you're looking to get your hands on a few famous, restaurant-inspired meals, we've curated the perfect meal list of recipes suited to fit any occasion!

1. Creamy Chicken

A quick and easy recipe to start this chapter off makes pan-fried, creamy chicken breast pieces. It'll take less than half an hour from start to finish, and is perfect for any lunch/dinner plans!

Prep Time: 10 minutes

Cooking Time: 20 minutes

Nutritional Facts/Info:		
4 Servings	Per Serving	
Calories	176	

Carbs	5g	
Fat	4g	
Protein	26g	

Ingredients:

- 4 chicken breasts (butterfly them in half/pound the breast pieces to ½ inch in width)
- 2 tsp of onion powder
- 2 tsp of ginger and garlic paste/garlic paste
- 2 tsp of chopped parsley, divided
- 1 tsp of thyme
- 1 tsp of rosemary
- ½ tsp of turmeric
- 3 tbsps of garlic paste or 2 cloves of garlic, minced
- 1 cup of milk
- salt and pepper to taste (about 1 tsp of each)
- 1 tsp of cornstarch mixed with 1 tbsp of water

Directions:

1. In a large pan, drizzle 1 tbsp of oil over medium-high heat. Place the chicken breasts flat in the pan and cover with the onion powder and 2 tsp of garlic paste. Sprinkle in some salt and pepper, and fry the chicken for 5 minutes on either side (if the chicken breasts are

thicker, cook for longer). Set the chicken aside once cooked.

2. Pour 2 more tsps of oil into the frying pan and add in the 3 tbsps of garlic paste,1 tsp of parsley, thyme, and rosemary and stir over the heat for about 1 minute, until the aromas of the herbs and spices are awakened.

3. Slowly pour the milk into the pan and season with salt and pepper. Raise the heat, bringing the contents to a boil and stir the cornstarch into the pan. Stir until the sauce begins to thicken, then lower the heat and allow it to simmer for about 1 minute.

4. Place the chicken breasts in the pan and leave to heat for another 2 minutes. Garnish with parsley and serve.

2. Stir Fried Chicken

Originating in China, stir fry is another great way to enjoy a meal, with or without carbs involved! It's high in protein and you get a great amount of vegetable intake too – plus, stir frying is a healthy way to fry your vegetables as it requires a small amount of oil, therefore the fat content is kept low.

Prep Time: 15 minutes

Cooking Time: 10 minutes

Nutritional Facts/Info:		
4 Servings	Per Serving	
Calories	343	
Carbs	29g	
Fat	13g	
Protein	26g	

Ingredients:

- 1 lb of chicken breasts, cut into thin strips/1 inch cubes
- 2 tbsps of olive oil
- 2 cups of broccoli florets
- ½ yellow bell pepper, cut into thin, short strips
- ½ red bell pepper, cut into thin, short strips
- ½ a cup of baby carrots, sliced lengthwise
- 2 tsp of ginger and garlic paste, divided
- 2 tsp of chili flakes, divided
- 1 tbsp of cornstarch
- ¼ cup of soy sauce
- ¼ cup of raw honey
- 1 tbsp of sesame oil
- salt and pepper to taste

Directions:

1. Whisk together the cornstarch and 2 tbsps of water in a small bowl, then combine the chicken broth, soy sauce, honey, sesame oil and 1 tsp of chili flakes. Whisk until well combined.

2. In a large pan/wok, heat 1 tbsp of oil over medium-high heat. Add the chicken into the wok and sprinkle some salt, pepper, 1 tsp of garlic paste and chili powder in. Fry for 5 minutes, stirring the seasoning to mix with the chicken.

3. Remove the chicken from the wok and lower the heat to a medium heat and add 1 more tbsp of oil into the pot.

4. Pour the broccoli, bell peppers and carrots into the wok and stir. Mix in the remainder of the ginger and garlic paste and cook until the vegetables are softened (about 3-4 minutes).

5. Bring the chicken pieces back into the wok and pour in the stir fry sauce that was made earlier. Stir the contents well to combine.

6. Raise the heat to a boil for 1 minute and stir. Serve hot.

3. Chicken Soup

A rich, creamy and aromatic protein-filled chicken soup is perfect for rainy days – metaphorically and literally! Whether it's pouring rain outside, or you're feeling a little under the weather, nothing is a better mood-lifter than a nice, spice-filled chicken soup! With anti-inflammatory ingredients like turmeric and garlic, and vitamin boosters like ginger and celery, this recipe will, without a doubt, get you out of the rainy day blues!

Prep Time: 10 minutes

Cooking Time: 35 minutes

Nutritional Facts/Info:		
6 Servings	Per Serving	
Calories	269	
Carbs	30.4g	
Fat	5.3g	
Protein	23.8g	

Ingredients:

- 2 tbsp of avocado/olive oil, divided
- 4 ½ tbsp of garlic paste, divided into 4 tbsp and ½ tbsp
- 1 yellow onion, sliced in thin strips
- 2 carrots, thinly sliced
- 1 tsp of ground turmeric
- 1 tbsp of grated ginger
- 6 cups of chicken broth
- 1 lb of chicken breast
- 1 tsp of chopped rosemary
- 1 tsp of chopped thyme
- black pepper and salt to taste
- 1 cup of Israeli couscous
- 2 cups of frozen peas

Directions:

1. First, prepare the chicken by cutting it into thin slices/1 inch squares. Place the chicken in a medium pan over medium-high heat with a drizzle of 1 tbsp olive oil. Sprinkle some salt and ½ a tbsp of garlic paste. Fry for 10 minutes (the chicken doesn't have to be fully cooked as it will be added back into the pot to cook). Set aside.
2. Next, place a medium-large pot over medium-high heat and add in the remaining oil. Drop the garlic, garlic paste and onion into the pot and fry until the onions have browned. Then add in the carrots and

celery and cook for another 2-3 minutes until the vegetables have softened.

3. Mix in the grated ginger and turmeric, and stir for 30 seconds. Add in the chicken broth, chicken breasts, rosemary, thyme, salt and pepper. Raise the heat and bring to a boil.

4. Pour in the couscous and stir – making sure that the chicken breast pieces are at the bottom of the pot, fully covered by the broth. Reduce heat to medium-low and allow to simmer for 15-20 minutes, allowing the chicken to fully cook.

5. Once the chicken is fully cooked, remove it from the pot and shred it with two forks. Add it back into the pot and pour in the frozen peas. Stir for 1 more minute and taste to adjust seasoning to your preference.

4. Chicken & Dumplings Stew

This meal is also extremely low on carbs and can act as a perfect light dinner option. It only takes about half an hour to prepare and cook, yet tastes mouthwateringly creamy and spicy.

Prep Time: 10 minutes

Cooking Time: 25 minutes

Nutritional Facts/Info:		
6 Servings	Per Serving	
Calories	716	
Carbs	53.1g	19%
Fat	34.8g	45%
Protein	45.8g	

Ingredients:

- 2 tbsp of oil
- 2 lbs of chicken breast, cubed/shredded
- 6 cups of chicken broth (alternatively you can use veg. broth for a less meaty flavor)
- 2 ½ cups all-purpose flour, divided into 2 cups & ½ a cup
- 2 cups of heavy cream, divided into 1 ½ cups and ½ a cup
- 1 cup of onion, diced
- 2 ½ tbsp of garlic paste
- 2 tsp of salt, divided
- 5 tbsp of butter
- 1 tsp of thyme

- 2 bay leaves
- 1 ½ cups of frozen peas
- 4 tbsps of parsley, finely chopped
- 1 tbsp of baking powder
- ½ tsp of pepper

Directions:

1. Drizzle some oil in a deep, medium-large pot and place over medium-high heat. Place the chicken in and ½ tsp of garlic paste and cook for 3-5 minutes, depending on the thickness of the meat. Remove the chicken and set aside.

2. Pour the carrots and onion into the pot and cook for 3 minutes, until softened. Mix in the remaining garlic and stir for another minute. Reduce the heat to low and pour in the butter and ½ a cup of flour and stir until lumps begin to form. Add the chicken back into the pot and stir to evenly coat the contents with the flour mix.

3. Pour the chicken broth, cream, thyme and bay leaves into the pot and sprinkle a bit of salt and pepper to taste. Leave the soup to simmer for a minute and then add in the frozen peas. Allow to simmer for 10 minutes.

4. While the soup is simmering, prepare the dumplings: Combine the remainder of flour, baking powder, salt, pepper and cream in a bowl and mix until it forms a dough.

5. Break pieces of dough into palm sized balls and roll in your hands, to form smooth 1 inch balls.

6. Add the balls into the soup and allow to simmer for another 15 minutes. Serve each bowl of soup with 2 dumplings.

5. Crumbed Chicken Tenders

Craving a little KFC or crumbed chicken? This recipe will satisfy all those cravings! If you want a more oily/fried taste, you can pop these tenders in a deep fry for 5 minutes, but this recipe will make use of the oven, for a healthier and less greasy alternative.

Prep Time: 15 minutes

Cooking Time: 15 minutes

Nutritional Facts/Info:		
4 Servings	Per Serving	
Calories	416	
Carbs	299g	10%
Fat	12g	18%
Protein	42g	84%

Ingredients:

- 1 ½ cups of breadcrumbs
- cooking spray/oil for drizzling
- 1 tsp of chilli spice (optional, if you'd like spicy breadcrumbs)
- 1 egg
- 1 tbsp of mayonnaise
- 1 ½ tbsp of Dijon mustard
- 2 tbsp of flour
- ½ tsp of salt
- ¼ tsp of black pepper
- 1 lb of chicken tenderloins/chicken breast, sliced into ⅔ inch slices

For homemade mustard sauce (mix well together):

- 1 tbsp of Dijon mustard
- 3 tbsp of mayonnaise
- ¼ tsp of pepper
- ½ tsp of salt

Directions:

1. Preheat your oven to 390°F and prepare a baking tray by spraying it with cooking spray/drizzle of oil. Evenly spread the breadcrumbs onto the tray and bake for 3 minutes (until golden brown). Set aside in a separate bowl, to cool down.

2. In a bowl, whisk together the 1 egg, mayonnaise, Dijon mustard, flour, salt and pepper until well combined.

3. Coat the baking tray with more cooking spray/another drizzle of oil.

4. Dip each chicken tender into the batter and then coat well in breadcrumbs. Place the tenders on the baking tray.

5. Bake for 15-20 minutes. Remove from the oven and serve with your favorite sauce/homemade mustard sauce.

6. Feta Stuffed, Garlic & Herb Chicken

This recipe is especially exciting for all the cheese lovers out there. Once prepared, it's a lovely meaty combination of herb chicken that oozes with melted, garlic-induced feta!

Prep Time: 15 minutes

Cooking Time: 20 minutes

Nutritional Facts/Info:		
4 Servings	Per Serving	
Calories	388	

Carbs	0.9g	0%
Fat	21.6g	28%
Protein	44.9g	

Ingredients:

- 4 chicken breasts
- 2 tbsp of ginger and garlic paste
- ½ cup of crumbled feta cheese
- salt and pepper to taste
- 1 tsp of mixed herbs
- 2 tbsp of oil
- 4 toothpicks

Directions:

1. Preheat the oven to 400°F and lightly drizzle a baking tray with oil.
2. Slit each chicken breast lengthwise to create a small pocket within the breast pieces.
3. Massage the breast pieces with garlic paste, working it into the meat.
4. In a small bowl, mix the feta, mixed herbs, salt and pepper. Use a spoon to scoop the cheese mix and fill each chicken breast and close the pockets by piercing a toothpick through it.
5. Place in the oven and cook for 20 minutes.

7. Butter Chicken

Sticking with the creamy chicken theme, butter chicken is a delicious mix of spice, cream and chicken. Originated in India, butter chicken is a quick dish of cubed chicken breasts, rich in butter and cream.

Prep Time: 5 minutes

Cooking Time: 15 minutes

Nutritional Facts/Info:		
4 Serving	Per Serving	
Calories	772	
Carbs	49.7g	18%
Fat	27.1g	35%
Protein	78.5g	

Ingredients:

- 3 chicken breasts, chopped into 1 inch squares
- 1 onion, diced
- 1 ½ tbsp of ginger & garlic paste

- 1 can of tomato paste (alternatively, you can blend 1 whole tomato into a puree)
- 1 tbsp of oil
- 1 tbsp of butter
- 1 cup of heavy cream
- 1 tbsp of garam masala
- 1 tsp of chili powder
- 1 tsp of Fenugreek (alternatively, you can use mustard seeds)
- 1 tsp of cumin
- 1 ½ tsp of salt
- cooked rice/naan for serving

Directions:

1. In a large pan/skillet, heat your oil, butter and onions over a medium-high heat until the onions soften and brown. Pour in the ginger & garlic paste and stir for 30 seconds, then incorporate your spices: cumin, chili powder, fenugreek, salt and garam masala and stir for another 30 seconds, until the aroma of the spices awaken.
2. Stir in your chicken breast cubes and tomato paste and cook for 5-6 minutes.
3. Incorporate the heavy cream, cover the pot if it has a lid, and allow to simmer for 10 minutes, stirring occasionally.

4. Serve with rice, naan or quinoa.

8. Spicy Chicken Tandoori

Originally, Tandoori was prepared over a fire heat (which is when the flavors and crispness is really prominent), so preparing a Tandoori dish for a barbecue is a fantastic option. Alternatively, if you're just preparing it for a weeknight dinner, you can use your oven grill for a similar effect.

Note: For best flavor results, prepare the marinade mix and marinade the chicken at least 12-24 hours before cooking.

Prep Time: 10 minutes

Cooking Time: 40 minutes

Nutritional Facts/Info:		
5 Serving	Per Serving	
Calories	556	
Carbs	94.9g	35%
Fat	10g	13%
Protein		19g

Ingredients:

- 1 ½ cups of plain yogurt
- 2 tbsp of oil
- 1 ½ tbsp of lemon juice
- 2 ½ tbsp of garlic & ginger paste
- 3 tsp of garam masala
- 1.5 tbsp of chili powder
- 1 tsp of turmeric
- 2 tsp of cumin
- 2 ½ tsp of coriander
- 2 tsp of chili flakes (optional, if you'd like it extra spicy)
- 1-1½ tsp of salt (depending on your liking)
- 2 lbs of chicken thigh & drumstick pack

Mint yogurt side (optional):

- 1 cup of plain yogurt
- ½ cup mint leaves, finely chopped
- ⅓ cucumber, diced
- salt and pepper, to taste
- ½ tsp olive oil

Directions:

1. In a bowl, stir in the 1 ½ cups of plain yogurt, 2 tbsps of oil, lemon juice, garlic & ginger paste, garam masala, chili powder, chili flakes, turmeric, cumin, coriander and salt to taste. Mix the combination well, then using

a zip-lock bag, pour the mixture into the bag and place the chicken pieces in. Massage the juices and spices into the chicken, through the plastic bag and leave to marinade in the refrigerator for 12-24 hours.

2. Once the chicken has marinated, preheat your oven to 350°F and line a baking tray with foil, then drizzle a little oil over the foil.

3. Place the chicken pieces onto the foil (keep the remaining marinade in the bag) and roast for 15 minutes.

4. Turn the chicken pieces over and baste the chicken with the remaining marinade and drizzle a little bit of oil over the chicken, with a spoon/brush. Raise the heat to 450°F and roast for another 15 minutes.

5. While the chicken is roasting, prepare your rice/naan as well as the mint yogurt (optional). In a small bowl, mix together all the ingredients: yogurt, mint, cucumber, salt, pepper and olive oil and set aside.

Note: if you are barbecuing the chicken, use the same method with foil & marinade halfway through, until your chicken is crisp.

Chapter 6: Seafood

Seafood is another fantastic source of protein. In addition to being high in Omega 3, it's also an extremely versatile ingredient – from clams to shellfish to whole fish fillets, there are endless possibilities of incorporating seafood into your meals.

1. Clam Chowder

This recipe is a delicious mix of cream, bacon, butter and clams! It's such a budget friendly meal to make at home, and only takes 45 minutes to whip up!

Prep Time: 15 minutes

Cooking Time: 30 minutes

Nutritional Facts/Info:		
6 Serving	Per Serving	
Calories	226	
Carbs	25.4g	9%
Fat	10.3g	13%
Protein	8.4g	

Ingredients:

- 4 rashers of bacon, diced
- 2 cans of chopped clams, with the juice
- 2 potatoes chopped & diced
- 1 onion, diced
- 2 tbsps of butter
- 1 ½ tsps of garlic paste
- 1 cup of vegetable stock
- ½ tsp of thyme
- 3 tbsp of flour
- 1 cup of milk
- 1 bay leaf
- salt and pepper to taste
- 2 tbsps of chopped parsley

Directions:

1. Drizzle oil into a deep-set pot and bring to a medium-high heat. Pour the diced bacon in and cook until crispy brown (about 5 minutes), then remove and place on a paper towel.
2. Plop the butter into the pot and once melted, add in your garlic, onions, bay leaf, thyme, salt and pepper and stir for about 2 minutes until the onions brown.
3. Slowly whisk the flour into the pot, then whisk in the milk, vegetable stock and clam juice. Whisk for about 2

minutes until the sauce thickens, then add in the potatoes.

4. Bring the contents to a boil, then lower the heat to a simmer and allow to cook for 15 minutes.

5. Once the potatoes have softened, slowly stir the clams into the pot – checking the thickness of the soup as you pour them in. Only pour more clams in if the sauce is too thick. Stir for about 2-4 minutes.

6. Serve each bowl with bacon and parsley drizzled on top. Serve hot.

2. Portuguese-Style Seafood Stew

Portuguese people have really refined and perfected their way of preparing seafood. Distinctive, pungent herbs and spicy chili are some of the significant aromas and flavors you're guaranteed to experience when indulging in the cuisine.

Prep Time: 5 minutes

Cooking Time: 35 minutes

Nutritional Facts/Info:		
6 Servings	Per Serving	
Calories	413	

Carbs	34.9g	13%
Fat	14.2g	18%
Protein	34.8g	

Ingredients:

- 18 mussels, cleaned
- 2 lbs of haddock/cod filet, cut into 1 inch chunks
- ⅓ cup of olive oil
- ½ tsp of chili flakes
- 3 tbsp of garlic paste
- 2 onions, chopped
- 2 bay leaves, halved
- 1 can of whole tomatoes
- 2 lbs of potatoes, peeled & cut into 2 inch chunks
- 1 green bell pepper, chopped
- 1 cup of bottled clam juice
- ½ a cup of dry white wine
- 3 tbsp of cilantro, finely chopped
- 3 tbsp of parsley, finely chopped
- salt and pepper to taste

Directions:

1. Boil your potatoes by filing a large pot with water and a pinch of salt over high heat. Boil for 15 minutes, then drain and set the potatoes aside.
2. In a medium pot over medium-high heat, lightly coat the surface with a drizzle of oil. Stir in the tomatoes, chili flakes, garlic paste, onions, bay leaves and pepper. Cook for about 12 minutes, stirring regularly.
3. Pour in the fish stock, wine, salt and pepper. Stir and cook for an additional 5 minutes.
4. Mix the mussels into the pot, cover with a lid and leave to cook for 5 minutes, until the mussels have opened up. Mix in the haddock/cod chunks, stir well to mix the sauce and leave to stew for 5-6 more minutes.
5. You can now stir the potatoes into the stew so that they absorb more flavor, or serve separately.
6. When serving, garnish with parsley and cilantro for an extra earthy, pungent taste.

3. Crumbed Fish

This quick 10 minute recipe is both healthy and delicious – offering a cheesy parmesan, garlic and crumbed taste to your fish filets. The best part is that you can use any fish for this recipe!

Prep Time: 5 minutes

Cooking Time: 7-10 minutes

Nutritional Facts/Info:		
2 Servings	Per Serving	
Calories	347	
Carbs	5.8g	2%
Fat	15.9g	20%
Protein	43.9g	

Ingredients:

- 2 white fish filets
- 2 tbsp of Dijon mustard
- 2 tbsps of olive oil, divided
- salt and pepper to taste
- ½ a cup of breadcrumbs
- 1 tbsp of parsley, chopped
- ⅓ cup of grated parmesan
- 1 tbsp of garlic paste
- 4 lemon wedges (optional)

Directions:

1. Set your oven to 390°F to preheat and set to broiler.
2. In a boil, mix the crumb ingredients: breadcrumbs, 1 tbsp of parsley, grated parmesan, garlic mix, 1 tbsp of olive oil and a pinch of salt.
3. Lightly drizzle oil on a baking tray and place the fish filets on it, sprinkle them with salt and pepper, then coat a layer of mustard on the top sides of the fish.
4. Sprinkle the breadcrumb mixture onto the mustard side of both the filets and gently press the crumbs into the fish. Drizzle oil over the tops of the fish and place in the oven for 10-12 minutes, then set the broiler to high and leave it in for an extra minute. Serve with a few lemon wedges for the best result.

4. Honey Glazed Salmon

This honey-glazed salmon recipe is extremely quick to make, yields a good amount of servings, is sweet and tart from the honey-vinegar mixture, and is extremely high in Omega 3 and protein!

Prep Time: 7 minutes

Cooking Time: 20-25 minutes

Nutritional Facts/Info:		
4 Servings	Per Serving	
Calories	218	
Carbs	9.5g	3%
Fat	10.5g	13%
Protein	22.2g	

Ingredients:

- 1 lb of salmon, cleaned & deskinned
- 2 tbsps of honey
- 2 tbsps of apple cider vinegar
- 2 tbsps of oil, divided
- 1 ½ tbsps of garlic paste
- 1 tsp of parsley
- ¼ tsp of chili flakes
- ⅓ tsp of mustard seeds (optional)
- ½ tsp of sesame seeds
- 1 tsp of salt
- a pinch of black pepper

Directions:

1. Preheat your oven to 375ºF and prepare a baking tray/oven dish, lining the surface of it with foil. Drizzle 1 tbsp of oil over the foil and place the salmon in the center of the tray.

2. In a small bowl, stir together your honey, vinegar, remaining oil, garlic paste, parsley, chili powder, salt and pepper. Pour the mixture evenly over the salmon – making sure that the salmon is nicely coated.

3. Sprinkle the mustard and sesame seeds over the top.

4. Pop the fish in the oven and bake for 20 minutes: Check on the salmon by prodding the center (or thickest) part of the meat with a fork – if it starts to flake, it is ready.

5. Tuna & Black Bean Burger Patties

This recipe is an amazing boost of lean protein, especially for pescatarians!

Prep Time: 10 minutes

Cooking Time: 5 minutes

Nutritional Facts/Info:		
4 Serving	Per Serving	

Calories	198	
Carbs	11.1g	4%
Fat	10.7g	14%
Protein	13.9g	

Ingredients:

- 1 can of light, shredded tuna
- ½ a cup of black beans, drained
- ⅓ cup of all-purpose flour
- 2 tbsps of oil
- ½ tbsp of black pepper
- ¼ onion, diced

Directions:

1. In a bowl, pour in the black beans and mash it with a fork, until smooth. Add in the tuna, onions and pepper and mix well.
2. Slowly pour in the flour while mixing the contents, so that the contents all stick together, forming one massive clump. Divide the clump into 4 equal balls and flatten them using your hands to create patties.
3. Heat a small frying pan over medium heat and drizzle the oil into the pan. Fry each patty for about 4 minutes,

flipping halfway through. The patties should turn a dark brown on either side.

4. Serve them in burger buns with your favorite toppings, or enjoy it in a couscous/quinoa salad!

6. Tempura Fried Prawns

The crispy delicacy of tempura prawns originated in Japan, but it is now a worldwide favorite. Tempura frying batter can also be used on other seafood sources, such as scallops or squid.

Prep Time: 15 minutes

Cooking Time: 10 minutes

Nutritional Facts/Info:		
2 Servings	Per Serving	
Calories	367	
Carbs	38g	
Fat	21g	
Protein	18.5g	

Ingredients:

- 4 prawns (deveined & cleaned)
- 4 slices of sweet potato
- 2 slices of renkon (alternatively, you can use other vegetables)
- 2 slices of shiso
- 50g of all-purpose flour
- 1 tbsp of mayonnaise
- oil, for frying

For homemade Tentsuyu dipping sauce (optional)

- ½ tbsp of Dashi powder
- ¼ cup of Mirin
- ¼ cup of Soy sauce
- ¼ cup of grated daikon

Directions:

1. Wash, cut and clean your prawns and vegetables.
2. In a bowl, combine the flour with 2 ½ oz of water, and 1 tbsp of mayonnaise. Mix well and place in the refrigerator for later.
3. In a deep pan/skillet fill it to about ⅓ with oil and bring to a medium-high heat.
4. Once the oil has heated up (little bubbles should form on the surface), take your flour batter out of the fridge

and dip your vegetables and prawns into the batter, coating them well.

5. Fry the vegetables and prawns in the oil (make sure they do not touch each other), for about 3-5 minutes for each item. The batter should turn a golden brown, this will indicate its readiness.

6. Place the contents on a paper towel to drain out the extra oil.

7. To make the dipping sauce: heat a small pan over the stove on high heat. Pour in the mirin sauce and bring to boil for 1 minute. Stir in 1 cup of water, soy sauce and dashi powder, bring the mixture to a boil. Pour the sauce into a small bowl and allow to cool down. Garnish each serving of Tentsuyu dipping sauce with 1 tbsp of daikon and serve with Tempura.

7. Sushi

One of the many reasons why homemade sushi is amazing, is that you get so much more sushi for the cost factor! Plus, once you master the basic art of sushi making, you can experiment with so many different kinds and styles!

Prep Time: 15 minutes

Cooking Time: 20 minutes + cooling time for the sushi rice

Nutritional Facts/Info:		
6 rolls (serves approx. 3)	Per Serving	
Calories	359	
Carbs	21.6g	8%
Fat	25.9g	33%
Protein	11.9g	

Ingredients:

- 6 sheets of seaweed
- 1 1/2 cups of sushi rice
- ½ lb of raw salmon/tuna, thinly sliced
- 4 oz of cream cheese
- 1 avocado, cut into thin slices
- 1 carrot, cut into short, thin slices
- 1 tbsp of mayonnaise
- soy sauce, wasabi & ginger for serving

Directions:

1. Boil your sushi rice in ½ a pot of water for about 20 minutes. Drain the rice through a sieve and set it aside to cool down.

2. Prepare your working station: Lay out the sliced avocado, sliced carrot, cream cheese and sliced fish around the station. Get a glass of water ready and place a tablespoon in it.

3. Lay out one sheet of seaweed, with the shinier side on the bottom. Using the wet tablespoon, smear sushi rice over ¾ of the seaweed sheet, leaving 1 inch of the seaweed bare.

4. 1 inch into the rice, layer slices of fish, carrot, avocado and a dollop of cream cheese. Roll the seaweed tightly and once you reach the end, wet your fingertips and pat it on the seaweed (so that it becomes sticky) and stick the seaweed to the roll, tightly closing it.

5. Using a sharp knife, cut the roll in half, then again, until it is in 8 equal small rolls.

6. Repeat the process until the contents are finished. Alternatively, you can make sashimi and/or nigiri with the remaining contents.

7. Place a dollop of mayonnaise on each sushi roll and serve with soy sauce, wasabi and ginger.

8. Seared Scallops with Coconut Lemongrass Sauce

This zesty summer dish is perfect as an appetizer or as served as a full meal, when paired with rice or couscous. The only cooking that has to take place is to sear the scallops/shrimp (whichever you have available), but other than this, it is a quick, healthy and refreshing Thai-style option!

Prep Time: 10 minutes

Cooking Time: 15 minutes

Nutritional Facts/Info:		
4 Servings	Per Serving	
Calories	514	
Carbs	41.6g	15%
Fat	23g	30%
Protein	35.3g	

Ingredients:

- 1 lb of scallops/shrimp
- 1 shallot, diced

- 1 tbsp of coconut oil
- 4 tbsps of white vinegar
- 1 lime (zest & juice)
- 1 stalk of lemongrass, smashed
- 2 slices of ginger
- 1 can of coconut milk
- 1 ½ tsps of fish sauce
- ½ tsp of chili flakes/1 red chili chopped finely
- salt and pepper to taste
- a handful of basil leaves, chopped thinly
- rice/couscous for meal serving
- sriracha sauce (optional)

Directions:

1. Set the rice/couscous to cook while you prep the rest of the meal.
2. Heat up the vinegar in a small pan and toss in the shallots, leave on low heat for 5 minutes, until the vinegar reduces. Pour in the coconut milk, ½ of the lime zest, lemongrass and ginger. Stir to combine the flavors and leave to simmer for 5 minutes.
3. Next, pour in the fish sauce, 1 tbsp of lime juice and chili flakes. Remove the mixture from heat and set aside.

4. Wash and pat dry your scallops/shrimp (make sure you've cleaned and deveined them too). Season the scallops with salt and pepper.

5. Heat up a skillet with coconut oil over medium heat and then place the scallops in, searing them for 2-3 minutes on either side.

6. Serve the scallops with couscous/rice and drizzle the sauce over, alternatively you can enjoy the scallops & sauce alone. Garnish with basil, lime zest and a drop of sriracha for the extra spicy kick!

Chapter 7: Sauce & Dressing

Adding that little extra touch to each meal, homemade sauces & dressings are literally the cherry on the top! Here are a few recipes from around the world that add those little extra touches to our meals!

1. 2-Ingredient Tahini Paste

Tahini paste is believed to originate from Israel, but has been an ever-growing popular paste and addition to meals around the world. It consists mainly of sesame seeds and has a salty, nutty, oily taste and aroma. It's an extremely healthy source of fats and antioxidants, so it's definitely worth adding to a few dishes per week!

Prep Time: 15 minutes

Cooking Time: 30 minutes

Nutritional Facts/Info:		
16 Tablespoons	Per Tbsp	
Calories	36	
Carbs	2g	

Fat	7g	
Protein	1g	

Ingredients:

- 1 cup of hulled sesame seeds
- 3 tbsps extra virgin olive oil (or more, if you prefer an oilier paste)

Directions:

1. Pour the sesame seeds into a pan and roast over medium-high heat, stirring regularly, until the seeds are brown.
2. Allow the seeds to cool then place them in a blender/food processor. Drizzle in 3 tbsps of olive oil and process until a paste is formed. Slowly add in more oil until you reach the consistency you'd prefer.
3. Thoroughly stir the paste before storing the tahini in an airtight jar/container and place in the refrigerator. Tahini can be stored for about 3 months.

2. Spicy Mexican Barbecue Sauce

This spicy, Mexican inspired barbecue sauce can accompany any dish, to add that extra heat. As it incorporates beer in the recipe, it's especially special for barbecue meals!

Prep Time: 15 minutes

Cooking Time: 15 minutes

Nutritional Facts/Info:		
12 Servings	Per Serving	
Calories	126	
Carbs	5.8g	2%
Fat	11.6g	15%
Protein	0.7g	

Ingredients:

- ⅔ olive oil
- 1 onion, diced
- ½ tbsp garlic paste
- 1 ½ tsps of salt
- 1 chili pepper, seeded & diced

- 2 tomatoes, peeled & chopped
- 2 tbsps of chili powder
- 2 tbsps of sugar
- ¼ cup of vinegar
- ¼ cup of beer

Directions:

1. Heat oil in a pan over medium heat. Drop in the onions and fry until browned.
2. Stir in the garlic, chili, chili powder, salt and tomatoes. Allow it to simmer for 3-5 minutes until the mixture thickens.
3. Pour in the sugar, vinegar and beer and let it simmer for 10 minutes, stirring regularly. Remove from heat and let it cool.

3. Tangy French Remoulade Sauce

If you're looking for an interesting tart sauce to accompany your meal, this remoulade sauce is a fantastic option! Originated in France, it's prominently known for its tangy mayonnaise, capers and herbs mixture.

Prep Time: 15 minutes

Cooking Time: 15 minutes

Nutritional Facts/Info:		
8 Servings	Per Serving	
Calories	146	
Carbs	1g	
Fat	16g	
Protein	0g	

Ingredients:

- ¾ cup of mayonnaise
- 1 ½ tbsp of cornichon or dill relish
- 1 tsp of finely chopped capers
- 1 tbsp of lemon juice
- 1 tbsp of mustard (preferably Dijon)
- 2 tsp of chopped parsley
- 1 dash of hot sauce
- ½ tsp of salt

Directions:

1. In a bowl, mix the mayonnaise with the cornichon, capers, lemon juice, mustard, salt and parsley together.
2. Stir in the hot sauce and then cover with plastic wrap. Place in the refrigerator until needed.

4. Duck Sauce

Duck sauce is a famous condiment that originated in China, which is usually used to accompany duck and chicken meals – thus its name. Its prominent ingredients include plums, apricots, peaches and vinegar. It's a sweet, high-fructose dressing that works well with glazed meat.

Prep Time: 5 minutes

Cooking Time: 2 minutes

Nutritional Facts/Info:		
4 Servings	Per Serving	
Calories	53	
Carbs	14g	
Fat	1g	
Protein	1g	

Ingredients:

- 2 tsps of sugar
- 1 ½ tbsps of hot water
- 3 tbsps of apricot preservatives

- 1 salted pickled plum (pitted)
- ½ a tsp of juice from pickled plum
- ⅛ tsp of soy sauce
- ¼ tsp of rice vinegar

Directions:

1. Stir the sugar and hot water together in a bowl, until the sugar is dissolved.
2. Add the apricot preserves and plum into the bowl and stir with a fork to break up the contents.
3. Pour in the remaining ingredients: juice from the pickled plum, soy sauce and vinegar. Stir well and then leave the sauce to sit for 5 minutes. Stir one last time and then serve. You can store duck sauce for several months.

5. Spicy Jamaican Jerk Sauce

Scotch bonnet peppers, thyme and garlic are a few prominent ingredients and flavors that you'll certainly pick up on, in a Jamaican Jerk Sauce. It's famously known as quite a spicy sauce that brings that special kick out in the meaty meals it accompanies.

Prep Time: 15 minutes

Cooking Time: 2 minutes

Nutritional Facts/Info:		
8 Servings	Per Serving	
Calories	101	
Carbs	25g	
Fat	1g	
Protein	2g	

Ingredients:

- ½ cup of ground allspice
- ½ cup of brown sugar
- 6 garlic cloves
- 4-6 scotch bonnet peppers (seeded and cored)
- 1 tbsp of thyme
- 2 bunches of scallions
- 1 tsp of cinnamon
- ½ tsp of nutmeg
- salt and pepper to taste
- 2 tbsps of soy sauce

Directions:

1. Combine all of the ingredients in a blender/food processor and blend until smooth. Enjoy!

6. Creamy Mushroom Sauce

Perfecting a creamy mushroom sauce is another perfect addition to the dinner table – adding that little rich and creamy taste to a pasta dish, steak or roast.

Prep Time: 5 minutes

Cooking Time: 15 minutes

Nutritional Facts/Info:		
6 Servings	Per Serving	
Calories	132	
Carbs	11g	
Fat	8g	
Protein	5g	

Ingredients:

- 1 tbsp of butter
- 2 tbsps of oil
- 5 cups of portobello mushrooms, halved
- 2 sprigs of thyme
- 1 tbsp of garlic paste

- 1 cup of cream
- 1 cup of milk
- 3 tsps of flour
- 1 tbsp of lemon juice
- salt and pepper to taste
- 2 tbsps of parsley, chopped

Directions:

1. In a small bowl, mix together the flour and milk, until the mixture is thick and sticky.
2. In a pan, combine the butter and oil and heat over medium heat. Once the butter has melted, add in the mushrooms and garlic and stir for about 5 minutes, ensuring that the mushrooms darken in color.
3. Pour the cream and milk into the pan and leave to simmer for 8 minutes, stirring regularly.
4. Sprinkle in your salt, pepper and lemon and taste, adding more if desired. Garnish with parsley and serve.

7. Thai Satay Peanut Sauce

Peanut sauce is a perfect condiment for any meal. It can also be turned into a vegan sauce, which will add a great protein addition to vegan meals.

Prep Time: 18 minutes

Cooking Time:2 minutes

Nutritional Facts/Info:		
4 Servings as a dip	Per Serving	
Calories	237	
Carbs	17g	
Fat	17g	
Protein	9g	

Ingredients:

- 1 cup of roasted, unsalted peanuts
- ⅓ cup of water
- 1 tbsp of garlic paste/2 cloves of garlic, minced (if you'd like a chunkier paste)

- ½ tsp of soy sauce
- 2 tsps of sesame oil
- 1 tbsp of brown sugar
- 2 tbsps of fish sauce (which can be substituted for 2 ½ tbsps of soy sauce for vegetarians)
- ½ tsp of tamarind paste
- 2 tbsps of lime juice
- ½ tsp of cayenne pepper
- ⅓ coconut milk
- ½ a green chili, chopped (if you'd like extra spice)

Directions:

1. Add all the ingredients into a blender/food processor and blend until a smooth paste. Pour in more coconut milk if you desire a thinner, runnier paste and blend more.
2. When serving, you can drizzle a little olive oil in the center of the paste to keep the paste nice and moist.

8. Caramel Sauce

This delicious and easy recipe yields up to 2 cups and is perfect for if you're craving something sweet and want to whip up a quick treat with basic pantry ingredients.

Prep Time: 8 minutes

Cooking Time: 8 minutes

Nutritional Facts/Info:		
12 Servings (2 cups)	Per Serving	
Calories	123	
Carbs	24g	
Fat	3g	
Protein	1g	

Ingredients:

- 1 ½ cups of brown sugar
- 4 tbsps of all-purpose flour
- 1 cup of boiling water
- a pinch of salt (½ tsp)
- 2 tbsps of butter
- 2 tbsps of heavy cream
- vanilla (optional, to taste)

Directions:

1. Heat a pan over medium-high heat and mix together the flour and sugar, stirring well.

2. Once the contents have mixed well, stir in the water & salt. Allow to cook for 6 minutes, stirring regularly so that the sugar is well blended. If the mix gets too thick, slowly mix more water in.

3. Remove from heat and mix in the butter, cream and vanilla. Stir well to mix and melt all the ingredients together.

Chapter 8: Takeaway

Takeaway is always a great way to explore different cuisines/meals and satisfy your cravings. What would you do if you knew you could do that from the comfort of your own home? From Chick-Fil-A to Kung Pao, this list of famous restaurant copycat meals will not only satisfy your cravings, but your wallet as well!

1. Homemade Big Macs

Craving a juicy, meaty Big Mac? It's a rather simple combination of a burger, but the special secrets lie in the meat patties, sauce and the vital ingredients: pickles and sesame seed buns!

Prep Time: 15 minutes

Cooking Time: 30 minutes

Nutritional Facts/Info:		
1 Serving	Per Serving	
Calories	712	
Carbs	67.1g	24%

Fat	31g	40%
Protein	47.4g	

Ingredients:

- 3 oz of ground beef
- ¼ cup of onion, diced
- 1 tsp of finely grated onion/onion powder
- 1 ½ tbsps of mayonnaise
- 1 ½ of pickle relish
- 1 tsp of yellow mustard
- 1 tsp of sugar
- ¼ tsp of Marmite
- ¼ tsp of turmeric
- 1 egg white
- 1 sesame seeded burger bun
- ¼ cup of shredded lettuce
- 4 pickle slices
- salt and pepper to taste
- 1 cheese square

Directions:

1. Divide the ground beef into two balls, then flatten into burger patties. Place on a plate, layered with parchment paper and place in the refrigerator.

2. In a small microwave safe bowl, place two layers of paper towels and pour in the ¼ cup of diced onion. Microwave for 8-10 minutes, until the onions have dehydrated.

3. While the onions are in the microwave, in a separate bowl, stir together the mayonnaise, relish, mustard, sugar, Marmite and turmeric, mixing well. Place in the refrigerator.

4. Cut the burger bun in half and heat up a pan over the stove, to medium heat. Lightly coat the bun in egg white and place the bun on the pan, to toast then set aside.

5. Remove the patties from the refrigerator and season with salt and pepper. Using the same heated pan, place the patties onto the pan and fry for 1 minute on either side – flipping with a spatula. Add the layer of cheese over one of the patties and fry for 1 more minute.

6. While the patties are fry, begin layering your burger: Spread the mayonnaise sauce on both halves of the bun, then layer on the dried onions and pickles. Then place the patties into the burger and close. Serve hot.

2. The Double Shack Stack

In keeping with the fast-food burger theme, another delicious option is the mushroom and double beef patty burger that gloriously reigns down from Shake Shack heaven!

Prep Time: 30 minutes

Cooking Time: 15 minutes

Nutritional Facts/Info:		
2 Servings (burgers)	Per Serving	
Calories	1430	
Carbs	125.3	46%
Fat	52.2g	67%
Protein	116.3g	

Ingredients:

- 1 lb ground beef
- 4 portobello mushrooms, cleaned and stems removed
- 2 oz of grated cheese (muenster preferably)
- 2 oz of grated cheddar cheese

- 1 cup of all-purpose flour
- 2 eggs, beaten
- 1 cup of breadcrumbs
- 1 quart of peanut oil (for frying)
- salt and pepper to taste
- ½ tsp of vegetable oil
- 4 squares of cheese
- 2 Sandwich-sized burger rolls, toasted in butter
- 2 tbsps of shack sauce, or a tangy, mayonnaise condiment
- 2 lettuce leaves
- 4 slices of tomato

Directions:

1. Divide the beef into 2 equal patties and store in the refrigerator.
2. If you have a steamer, steam the mushrooms for about 10 minutes. Alternatively, place the mushrooms on 3 layers of paper towel, lay it on the microwave plate and microwave for 4 minutes. Then let the mushrooms cool down on the paper towel, allowing the moisture to drain from them.
3. In a separate bowl, mix together the cheeses and then scoop half of the cheese into one mushroom cap, and the other half into the other. Gently press the contents into the mushrooms so that they are well compressed.

4. Coat each mushroom in flour and then dip in egg white, then coat the mushroom patties in breadcrumbs.

5. Fill a pan with peanut oil and bring to a high heat. Fry the mushroom patties for 2 minutes on either side, until golden brown. Transfer the patties to a paper towel and season with salt.

6. In a separate skillet, drizzle with vegetable oil and fry the beef patties. Season with salt whilst frying and use a spatula to press down on the patties. Fry for about 2 minutes on either side until brown and crusty.

7. Top each patty with 1 slice of cheese and let it sizzle for 1 more minute.

8. In the meantime, start arranging your burgers: Spread the sauce on both halves of each burger bun, place 1 lettuce leaf and then 2 tomatoes. Layer on 1 beef patty, then the mushroom patty, then cover with the second beef patty. Close the burgers and serve hot.

3. In-N-Out Double Double Trouble

And one last famous burger that we just can't get enough of? The famous In-N-Out style beef burger! The sauciest, juiciest of them all, consisting of relish, onions and mustard – this burger will surely fulfil all your fast-food cravings!

Prep Time: 25 minutes

Cooking Time: 10 minutes

Nutritional Facts/Info:		
2 Servings (burgers)	Per Serving	
Calories	961	
Carbs	64.8g	24%
Fat	54.6g	70%
Protein	52.9g	

Ingredients:

- ½ lb of beef chopped into 1-inch cubes
- 2 tsps of vegetable oil, divided
- 1 onion, finely chopped
- 2 tbsps & 2 tsps of mayonnaise
- 1 tbsp of ketchup
- 2 tsps of relish
- ½ tsp of sugar
- ½ tsp of white vinegar
- 2 burger buns
- 8 pickle chips
- 2 slices of tomato

- 2 lettuce leaves
- ¼ cup of mustard
- 4 cheese squares
- salt and pepper to taste

Directions:

1. Evenly place the meat chunks apart, on a tray (preferably) and chill in the freezer for about 10 minutes.

2. Once the meat has chilled, divide the meat into 2 equal parts and blend in a processor for about 10 seconds, until the meat is a medium-fine grind. Repeat for the second batch and refrigerate until ready to use.

3. Heat a pan over the stove on medium heat. Drizzle 1 tsp of oil in and fry the onions, adding a pinch of salt. Fry for 7-10 minutes until golden brown. Add 1 tsp of water to the onions and stir until the water has evaporated, repeat this process 3 times. Set the onions aside.

4. Drizzle ½ a tsp of oil back into the skillet. Cut the burger buns in half and place them flat down on the pan and leave them to toast for about 1 minute, until brown. Set aside.

5. In a small bowl, mix together the mayonnaise, ketchup, relish, sugar and vinegar. Stir well and set aside.

6. Remove the meat patties from the fridge, season with salt and pepper, and mold the meat into patties using

your hands. Place the same pan back onto the stove and pour the remainder of oil into the pan, raising the heat to a medium-high. Place the patties onto the pan and fry for 2 minutes on either side and flip using a spatula. While the patties cook, spread 1 tbsp of mustard on the raw side of each patty. Flip the patties over and then place a slice of cheese on each one, allowing it to cook for an additional minute.

7. Prepare the burgers: Spread both sides of each burger with the mayonnaise mix, place 4 pickles in each burger, 1 tomato slice and lettuce. Top each burger with the diced onions, then place 2 patties in each burger and close off the burgers. Serve hot.

4. Kung Pao Chicken & Peanut Stir Fry

Now to spice things up a little, this quick and wholesome recipe is the epitome of spicy, Thai-style stir fry! With a succulent sauce that ties it all together, this recipe is definitely worth a try, especially for the spice fanatics!

Prep Time: 10 minutes

Cooking Time: 15 minutes

Nutritional Facts/Info:		
4 Servings	Per Serving	
Calories	560	
Carbs	9.1g	3%
Fat	33.9g	44%
Protein	54.7g	

Ingredients:

Chicken prep:

- 1 ½ lbs of chicken breast/thigh pieces, cut into 1-inch chunks
- 1 tsp soy sauce
- 1 tsp of mirin
- ½ tsp of sugar
- ½ tsp of sesame oil
- ½ tsp of cornstarch
- salt and pepper to taste
- ½ tsp of garlic paste
- ½ tsp of chili flakes

Stir Fry:

- 1 tbsp of soy sauce
- 1 tbsp of mirin
- 1 tbsp of white vinegar
- 2 tbsps of chicken stock
- 1 tbsp of sugar
- 1 tsp of sesame oil
- 1 tsp of cornstarch
- 3 tbsps of oil
- 1 green bell pepper. diced
- 1 red bell pepper, diced
- 2 stalks of celery, diced
- ½ cup of roasted peanuts/cashews
- 2 tsps of garlic & ginger paste
- 1 scallion, finely chopped
- 8 small, dried red chili

Directions:

1. Marinade the chicken by combining all of the ingredients for the chicken into a medium bowl, mix well so that the spices and oils work their way into the meat. Cover and set aside for 20 minutes.

2. In a small bowl, mix together the soy sauce, mirin, vinegar, chicken stock, sugar, sesame oil and cornstarch into a bowl. Whisk together with a fork/whisk until ingredients are well combined.

3. In a wok, drizzle 1 tbsp of oil and place over high heat – the oil should start to sizzle/smoke. Place in the chicken and cook until the chicken has browned (about 3-5 minutes). Remove the chicken from the wok and set aside.
4. Pour the remainder of oil into the wok and toss in the bell peppers and celery and stir. After about 1 minute, mix in the peanuts and stir to combine.
5. Mix in the garlic and ginger paste, scallions, chilies and stir well into the vegetables, until the spicy aroma fills the air. Mix in the chicken and soy sauce and toss the contents so that the sauce mixes well and thickens. Stir for an additional minute and serve hot!

5. Starbucks Spinach & Feta Breakfast Wrap

Looking for something a little healthier? This Starbucks inspired spinach and feta wrap is a perfect, warm breakfast/brunch bite!

Prep Time: 2 minutes

Cooking Time: 8 minutes

Nutritional Facts/Info:		
1 Serving	Per Serving	
Calories	252	
Carbs	23.3g	8%
Fat	10.8g	17%
Protein	16.2g	

Ingredients:

- 1 whole-wheat tortilla
- ¼ cup of sliced mushrooms
- 2 cups of spinach
- 1 egg, whisked
- 2 tbsps of feta cheese
- 1 tbsp of chopped sundried tomatoes
- salt and pepper to taste

Directions:

1. Place a small pan over medium heat and warm the tortilla for about 1 minute, flipping halfway through. Plate the tortilla and set aside.
2. Drizzle the pan with a dash of oil/cooking spray and add in the mushrooms with a pinch of pepper and salt–

sauté the mushrooms for 2 minutes then add in the spinach, cooking for another minute, until wilted.

3. Pour in the whisked egg and stir, allowing to cook until the egg has set.

4. Place the contents from the pan into the tortilla, then sprinkle in the feta and sundried tomatoes. Fold the wrap over and enjoy!

6. Glazed Krispy Kreme Doughnuts

Ever crave the fresh, soft, sweet and syrupy goodness of Krispy Kreme's doughnuts? Well we finally have the perfect recipe for you to master the homemade version! It's a great way to satisfy the teatime cravings without having to leave home!

Prep Time: 1 hour 30 minutes (some time is allocated for the dough to rise)

Cooking Time: 10 minutes

Nutritional Facts/Info:		
6 Servings	Per Serving	
Calories	850	

Carbs	140.2g	51%
Fat	25.5g	
Protein	15.6g	

Ingredients:

- 2 packs of yeast (¼ oz)
- ¼ cup of water
- 1 ½ cups of room temperature milk
- ½ cup of sugar
- 1 tsp of salt
- 2 eggs
- ⅓ cup of shortening
- 5 cups of all-purpose flour
- oil for frying

For the glaze:

- ⅓ cup of butter
- 2 cups of powdered sugar
- 1 ½ tsp of vanilla
- 4-6 tsps of hot water

Directions:

1. In a medium-large bowl, combine the yeast with warm water and mix until it dissolves. Pour in the milk, sugar,

salt, eggs, shortening and 2 cups of flour and beat for 30 seconds on low, and an additional 2 minutes on medium speed. Slowly stir in the remaining 3 cups of flour and mix well. Cover the bowl and allow to rest for 1 hour.

2. When the dough is ready, lightly flour a working space and place the dough onto the flour. Sprinkle flour over the dough and roll the dough to about ½ inch in thickness.

3. Using a doughnut cutter/cup, cut circular shapes out – make sure to cut a hole in the center too. Cover the doughnut shapes and let it rise for an additional 30 minutes.

4. When the doughnuts are almost done rising, heat about ½ to ¾ of a pot with oil and bring to a high heat – the oil should bubble at the surface.

5. Place the doughnuts into the oil, using a spatula, and fry until golden brown (about 1 minute), then flip them over and fry the other side for another minute.

6. Place the doughnuts on a drip tray/paper towel so that the excess oil is drained out.

7. While the doughnuts cool down, melt the butter for the glaze in a medium pan. Remove the pan from heat and stir in the sugar and vanilla, then add 1 tbsp of water at a time, stirring slowly, until it reaches a thick, leaky consistency.

8. Pour the glaze over the doughnuts and let it cool for about 10 minutes.

7. French Toast Sticks

Made famous by Burger King, these crispy, sweet delights are a perfect brunch or tea time snack! It only takes a quick 15 minutes to prep, yet is delightfully scrumptious and the best part is that this recipe only requires basic ingredients!

Prep Time: 5 minutes

Cooking Time: 10 minutes

Nutritional Facts/Info:		
4 Servings	Per Serving	
Calories	301	
Carbs	55.5g	20%
Fat	5.3g	7%
Protein	13.8g	

Ingredients:

- 8 slices of whole-wheat bread

- ½ cup of egg beaters
- 8 tbsps of splenda/sugar
- 4 tsps of French Vanilla coffee creamer powder
- ½ tsp of vanilla extract
- ¼ tsp of butter extract
- a pinch of salt
- cooking spray
- maple syrup/honey for drizzling

Directions:

1. Toast the slices of bread and then cut each slice into 4 equal strips.
2. In a small bowl, mix the egg beaters, splenda, cinnamon, vanilla extract, butter extract and salt together. Whisk the mixture together until all the contents have dissolved.
3. In a saucepan, coat the bottom with cooking spray and bring to a medium-high heat.
4. While the pan heats up, individually soak each slice of bread in the mixture for about 10 seconds on either side and then place them into the pan to cook for about 3-5 minutes on either side, until crispy and golden brown.
5. Drizzle maple syrup and some cinnamon over the end product and enjoy it whilst warm!

8. Taco Bell Crunchwrap Supremes

This crunchy, cheesy glorious wonder is perfect for a quick lunch bite! It's incorporated with all the Mexican-style ingredients of sour cream, shredded cheese and tortilla chips! When serving, you can always add a scoop of guacamole for the whole experience.

Prep Time: 10 minutes

Cooking Time: 5 minutes

Nutritional Facts/Info:		
4 Servings	Per Serving	
Calories	404	
Carbs	15.5g	6%
Fat	18g	23%
Protein	43.6g	

Ingredients:

- 4 tortillas
- 1 lb of ground beef (you can substitute this for soya mince, if you're vegetarian)

- salt and pepper to taste
- 1 tsp of garlic & ginger paste
- ½ tsp of chili flakes (optional)
- oil for frying
- ½ bag of tortilla chips
- 2 tbsps of sour cream
- 1 cup of shredded cheddar cheese
- ½ cup of shredded lettuce
- 1 tomato, diced
- ½ cup of queso style cheese
- guacamole (optional) for serving

Directions:

1. Drizzle oil into a pan over medium-high heat and add in the beef. Season with salt, pepper and chili flakes and add the spoon of garlic paste. Break apart the mince and cook for about 5 minutes until browned, then set aside.
2. Warm up the tortillas in the pan, placing each on the pan for 10 seconds, then flipping.
3. Lay each tortilla out on a plate and remember to place all of the ingredients into the center of each wrap: Add a dollop of sour cream and evenly spread the mince into each tortilla. Add in the cheeses and sprinkle the tortilla chips over each. Pop each tortilla in the microwave for 10-15 seconds.

4. Add some lettuce and tomatoes into each tortilla.

5. Heat up the pan again and drizzle some oil/butter to lightly coat the pan. Fold the outer edges of the tortilla inwards so that the contents of the wrap are covered.

6. Place the wraps onto the pan and cook for about 3 minutes, then flip it over, cooking for another 3 minutes.

7. You can serve with guacamole and a dash of hot sauce over the top – serve hot!

9. Homemade Wendy's Chili

This spicy combo of peppers, chili, beans and beef mince is a great, versatile dish suited to any occasion – be it dinner parties or a quick bit for lunch. It's a delicious mixture originally concocted by Wendy's and only takes a few minutes to prep, and throw into a pot. Viola! You've got a spicy chili bowl!

Prep Time: 15 minutes

Cooking Time: 15 minutes

Nutritional Facts/Info:		
16 Servings (cups)	Per Serving	

Calories	492	
Carbs	75g	27%
Fat	5.5g	7%
Protein	37.1g	

Ingredients:

- 2 lbs of ground beef
- ½ tsp of garlic paste
- 2 tsps of salt, divided
- 1 tsp of pepper
- 4 cans of tomato sauce
- 2 cans of rinsed & drained pinto beans
- 2 cans of rinsed & drained kidney beans
- 2 cans of diced onion & tomato
- ½ tsp of onion powder
- 2 tsps of ground cumin
- 2 tbsps of chili powder
- 1 tbsp of paprika
- a pinch of chili flakes
- 1 cup of water
- ½ cup of parsley for garnish

Directions:

1. Heat a large, deep-set pot over medium heat and pour in the beef, 1 tsp of salt, pepper and garlic paste. Mix the ingredients until the mince has browned.

2. Drain the meat using a sieve and place the meat back into the pot. Add all the other ingredients into the pot and stir well. Bring the contents to a boil, then reduce the heat to a simmer.

3. Leave to simmer for 15 minutes.

4. Dish the chili into bowls and garnish with parsley. Serve hot.

10. Crumbed KFC

What would a homemade copycat recipe list be without the one and only crumbed, homemade KFC-style chicken? The crispy, crunchy batter has made KFC an age-old traditional success story and we finally have a homemade copycat recipe that's suited to fit these cravings!

Prep Time: 20 minutes

Cooking Time: 18 minutes

Nutritional Facts/Info:		
18 Servings	Per Serving	
Calories	213	
Carbs	3g	
Fat	5g	
Protein	38g	

Ingredients:

- 2 whole chickens, cut into pieces (thighs, wings, drumsticks etc.)
- 2 cups of all-purpose flour
- 2 tsp of salt
- 1 ½ tsp of thyme
- 1 ½ tsp of basil
- 4 tbsp of paprika
- 1 tsp of oregano
- 1 tbsp of celery salt
- 2 tbsp of garlic salt
- 1 tbsp of black pepper
- 3 tbsp of white pepper
- 1 tbsp of mustard powder

- 1 tbsp of ground ginger
- oil for frying (should fill ¾ of a deep-set pot)

Directions:

1. In a small bowl, combine all of your herbs and spices together, mixing well.
2. Get a large bowl out and pour the flour into it, then add in the spice mixture. Stir the ingredients together until well-integrated.
3. Preheat a deep-set pot filled with ¾ oil to medium-high on the stove.
4. Dip each piece of chicken in water, coating it well, then cover the pieces in the flour mixture then leave the chicken to set for about 10 minutes.
5. Once the oil has heated up, fry the chicken pieces for about 10 minutes each, until golden brown (the bigger the chicken piece, the longer it should fry for, so consider frying bigger pieces of meat like the thigh pieces for 15-18 minutes each).
6. Place the cooked pieces over a rack/on paper towel so that the excess oil drips out.

Chapter 9: Vegetarian

If vegetables are creatively used and well-spiced, they are so versatile and give so much value to a dish! Here are a few vegetarian recipes compiled to fit a few weeknight dinners and healthy lunch options! From curries to salads, there's so much room to explore when it comes to vegetarian meals!

1. Vegan Mushroom & Pecan Nut Wellington

Wellington dishes are a wholesome and homey meal for the whole family to enjoy! Usually, Wellingtons incorporate minced meat, but this recipe makes delicious use of mushrooms and pecan nuts. Not only is it a much lighter and healthier Wellington option, it's also vegan!

Prep Time: 5 minutes

Cooking Time: 10 minutes

Nutritional Facts/Info:		
10 Servings	Per Serving	
Calories	390	

Carbs	26.2g	10%
Fat	30.1g	39%
Protein	4.9g	10%

Ingredients:

- 2 tbsps of olive oil
- 2 lbs of mushrooms, sliced
- 1 onion, diced
- 4-5 garlic cloves
- 1 tbsp of chopped rosemary
- ¼ cup of sherry wine
- 1 tsp of balsamic vinegar
- 1 cup of chopped pecan nuts (you can substitute this for walnuts)
- 2 tsps of truffle oil
- ½ cup of cheese (optional)
- coconut oil for "egg washing"
- 2 sheets of vegan puff pastry (brought to room temperature)
- salt and pepper to taste

Directions:

1. In a large pan, heat your oil over a medium-high heat. Stir in the mushrooms, onions, garlic, salt and

rosemary. Sauté the mushrooms and then lower the heat and let the mushrooms cook for about 10 minutes until their juice has evaporated.

2. Once the juice has evaporated, pour in the sherry wine and balsamic vinegar and sauté the mushrooms until the liquids have evaporated again.

3. Stir in the pecans, pepper and truffle oil (and cheese, if you choose) into the pan and remove from heat. Allow the mix to cool down.

4. Line a baking tray with parchment paper and lay the puff pastry over the parchment. Layer half of the filling over the pastry down the center of the pastry and fold the pastry over (to create a roll). Repeat with a second pastry and the remaining filling.

5. "Egg wash" the pastries with coconut oil and using a knife, score the pastries in a cross-hatch design.

6. Place in the oven for 35-40 minutes.

2. Shepherd's Pie

Shepherd's pie is another famous, homey dish that usually makes use of minced meat, but this divine vegetarian twist will combat both the craving of a delicious homemade shepherd's pie and provide a good amount of protein intake!

Prep Time: 30 minutes

Cooking Time: 1 hour 15 minutes

Nutritional Facts/Info:		
8 Servings	Per Serving	
Calories	383	
Carbs	49.6g	40%
Fat	15.9g	20%
Protein	12.2g	24%

Ingredients:

- 2 ½ lbs of potatoes (or 5 cups of mashed potatoes, preferably)
- 4 tbsps of butter
- ½ a cup of plain yogurt
- ½ a cup of milk/heavy cream
- 2 tsps of curry powder
- salt and pepper to taste

For the filling:

- 2 ½ cooked lentils
- 2 tbsps of olive oil
- 1 onion, diced

- 2 tbsps of garlic paste
- 2 cups of diced carrots
- 2 cups of diced celery
- 2 tsps of garam masala
- 1 tsp of cumin
- 1 tsp of coriander
- 2 tsps of fenugreek leaves
- 1 cup of vegetable broth
- 1 cup of frozen peas
- salt and pepper to taste

For the gravy:

- 1 ¼ cups of warm vegetable broth
- 3 tbsps of flour
- 2 tbsps of olive oil
- 1 tsp of cumin seeds
- 1 tsp of fennel seeds

Directions:

1. If the potatoes aren't mashed, prepare the potatoes by chopping them in 1 inch chunks and boil in salted water over medium-low heat for 20 minutes, until potatoes are softened.
2. While the potatoes boil, prepare the lentils (if uncooked): Cook the lentils in salted water over low heat for 20 minutes.

3. In a large, ovenproof pan/skillet, heat your oil over medium heat and then fry the onions for about 2 minutes until softened. Then lower the heat to a medium-low and stir in the garlic, carrots, celery, salt, cumin, coriander, fenugreek and garam masala and cook for 5-7 minutes until the vegetables soften and the spices are fragrant.

4. Pour in the broth and bring the contents to a simmer for about 7-8 minutes.

5. Check on the potatoes and lentils, and drain the ingredients using a colander. Set aside to cool.

6. Prepare the gravy while the vegetables simmer: In a small pot, simmer the cumin & fennel seeds in a drizzle of oil over medium heat. Stir until golden brown, then whisk in the flour for 1 minute. Slowly whisk in the vegetable broth and mix together. Keep stirring for about 2-3 minutes until the gravy has thickened.

7. Preheat the oven to 350°F.

8. In a large, ovenproof dish, combine the gravy, lentils and vegetables together and mix in the peas.

9. Mash the potatoes and mix in some butter/oil and yogurt and season with salt to taste. Layer the mash over the top of the dish's contents.

10. Pop in the oven for 20 minutes, then set the oven to broiler and leave the dish to broil for an additional 2 minutes.

3. Beetroot & Goat Cheese Salad

This colorful, nutritious dish is a quick and light meal option, perfect for both a summer lunch or winter dinner! Its warm lentil contents provide a hearty touch to the beetroot salad and harmoniously offer a wholesome, zesty dish.

Prep Time: 10 minutes

Cooking Time: 40 minutes

Nutritional Facts/Info:		
2 Servings	Per Serving	
Calories	507	
Carbs	61.4g	20%
Fat	19.4g	30%
Protein	26g	52%

Ingredients:

- 2 cups of cooked lentils
- 3-4 beetroots
- ½ red onion, diced
- 2 tbsps of olive oil

- 4 cups of baby spinach
- 3 garlic cloves, chopped
- 2 tbsps of balsamic vinegar
- ¼ cup of goat cheese, crumbled
- 2 tbsps of basil

Directions:

1. Preheat the oven to 425°F.
2. Wash and cut the beetroots into 1 inch wedges, place on a baking tray and drizzle with oil. Pop the tray in the oven and roast for 20 minutes.
3. While the beetroot roasts, prepare a large pan over medium heat and lightly cover the surface with 2 tbsps of oil. Add in the onions and fry for 3 minutes. Lower the heat and mix in the garlic, cooking for an additional 2 minutes.
4. Bring the heat down to low and mix the spinach into the pan, along with a sprinkle of salt and pepper. Cook for 2 more minutes until the spinach has wilted.
5. Pour the lentils into the pan and gently mix the contents together.
6. Once the beetroots are ready, drizzle the balsamic vinegar over them and mix it well. Let it sit for about 2 minutes, allowing the vinegar to soak into the beetroot.
7. Plate the spinach and lentil mix and layer with beetroots. Sprinkle goat cheese over the top and serve.

4. Palak Paneer in Creamy Spinach Paste

Palak Paneer is an Indian dish in origin and holds a similar taste to halloumi. It offers a good amount of healthy protein!

Prep Time: 10 minutes

Cooking Time: 20 minutes

Nutritional Facts/Info:		
4 Servings	Per Serving	
Calories	301	
Carbs	55.5g	20%
Fat	5.3g	7%
Protein	13.8g	

Ingredients:

- 24 oz of paneer
- 1 ½ lbs of fresh spinach
- ¾ of plain yogurt
- 3 tbsps of ghee/butter
- 1 onion, diced
- 2 tbsps of ginger, chopped

- 1 tbsp of garlic paste
- 1 jalapeno/chili, chopped
- 2 tsps of cumin
- 2 tsps of coriander
- 2 tsps of garam masala
- 1 tsp of mustard seeds
- 1 cup of water
- ½ cup of cashews
- 1 tsp of salt
- ½ tsp of sugar

Directions:

1. Heat up the ghee/butter in a large pan over medium heat. Add in the paneer and season with salt and pepper. Fry until the paneer is golden brown. Once cooked, set the paneer aside and cover with foil.
2. Add 3 more tbsps of ghee into the pan and combine the onions, ginger, garlic and chilies and fry until the onions have browned – about 10 minutes.
3. Pour the spices into the pan: coriander, cumin, garam masala and mustard seeds, and fry for 2-3 minutes until fragrant. Pour in the spinach and 1 cup of water and lower the heat to a simmer.
4. Once the spinach has wilted, transfer the contents from the pan into a blender and pour in the yogurt, cashews, sugar and salt. Blend until smooth.

5. Place the blended spinach mix back into the pan and heat over a low heat, combining the paneer into the pan. Mix the contents well and serve.

5. Cauliflower & Mushroom Risotto

Cauliflower, as of late, has especially proven to be a fantastic substitute for a lot of different ingredients. In this dish, it perfectly mimics rice! It's a much more healthier substitute as well as a tastier one, and compliments the creamy, mushroom risotto perfectly!

Prep Time: 25 minutes

Cooking Time: 35 minutes

Nutritional Facts/Info:		
4 Servings	Per Serving	
Calories	300	
Carbs	19g	
Fat	21g	
Protein	10g	

Ingredients:

- 5 tbsps of olive oil, divided
- 6 cups of sliced mushrooms (cremini, preferably)
- 1 cup of onion, chopped finely
- 2 tsps of garlic paste
- 2 tsps of thyme
- ¼ cup of dry white wine
- 24 oz (8 cups) of riced cauliflower
- 1 cup of water
- ½ cup of vegetable stock
- salt and pepper to taste
- ¾ cup of shredded parmesan cheese, divided in half

Directions:

1. In a large pan, lightly coat the surface with 1 and ½ tbsps of oil and heat over medium heat. Pour the mushrooms into the pan and fry for 8-10 minutes, until browned. Set the mushrooms aside.

2. Drizzle another 1 ½ tbsps of oil into the pan and mix in the onion, garlic and thyme, stirring for about 5 minutes until the onions have softened. Then pour in the wine and stir for 90 seconds, next, mix in the cauliflower, water and stock. Cover the pan and leave to cook, stirring occasionally for about 10 minutes. Remove from heat when the cauliflower is tender and crispy.

3. Place 3 cups of cauliflower mix as well as some of the remaining liquid in the pan, into a blender and process for about 15 seconds, until smooth.
4. Stir the cauliflower puree, mushrooms and cheese into the pan again, bringing to a medium heat. Sprinkle salt and pepper to season. Cook until the cheese has melted.
5. Garnish with the remainder of cheese and serve.

Chapter 10: Beef & Pork

From perfecting a juicy steak to succulent, sweet and sticky pork chops – here are a few basic but delicious ways to prepare red meat! A lot of the tender juice and taste in red meat comes from how it is cooked, as well as the sauce that it is combined with. These quick recipes will surely have yours and your guests' tummies ready for second rounds!

1. Pan-Cooked Steak

Perfecting a juicy steak is easier than it looks! As gloriously, mouth-wateringly delicious as it is, this recipe only requires 4 extra ingredients!

Prep Time: 5 minutes

Cooking Time: 10 minutes

Nutritional Facts/Info:		
4 Servings	Per Serving	
Calories	219	
Carbs	0.6g	0.2%

Fat	17.2g	26.5%
Protein	14.7g	29.4%

Ingredients:

- 2 ribeye steaks (about 1 inch thick)
- 1 tsp of salt
- 3 tbsps of unsalted butter
- 3 smashed cloves of garlic (or 1 ½ tbsps of garlic paste)
- 3 rosemary/thyme sprigs

Directions:

1. Remove the steaks from the refrigerator at least 1 hour prior to cooking. Pat the steaks dry with a paper towel.
2. Lightly coat the steaks with salt – making sure both sides are well seasoned.
3. Place a large cast-iron pan over high heat and allow to preheat for about 10 minutes. Place the steaks in the pan and leave to cook for 1 minute, then flip. Leave to cook for 1 more minute then flip again. Do this for up to 4 minutes, flipping 4 times.
4. Pour in the butter, garlic and rosemary into the pan and use a spoon to baste the seasoned, melted butter over the steak. Flip the steak and baste again. Repeat

this process for about 6 minutes, until the steak is medium rare.

5. Plate the steaks and allow to rest for 5 minutes then transfer over to a cutting board and thinly slice the meat. Drizzle pan juice over the meat and serve immediately.

2. Beef Stroganoff

Beef Stroganoff is a dish that embodies what a homey meal is. It's a delicious, hearty mix of tender beef and mushrooms in a creamy sauce, served over a bed of mashed potatoes, rice or noodles.

Prep Time: 10 minutes

Cooking Time: 35 minutes

Nutritional Facts/Info:		
6 Servings	Per Serving	
Calories	473	
Carbs	36.7g	12.2%
Fat	24.9g	38.2%
Protein	25.9g	51.8%

All you will need is:

- 3 tbsps of butter, divided
- 8 oz of mushrooms, thinly sliced
- 1 onion, diced
- 2 cloves of garlic, finely chopped
- 1 lb of ground beef
- 3 tbsps of all-purpose flour
- 1 ¼ tsps of paprika
- 4 cups of beef broth
- 1 tbsp of Dijon mustard
- 8 oz of dried egg noodles
- ¾ cup of Greek yogurt
- salt and pepper to taste
- 1 tbsp of parsley leaves

Directions:

1. In a large, deep-set pot, melt 1 tbsp of butter over medium-high heat. Stir in the mushrooms and sprinkle salt and pepper to taste. Fry the mushrooms for about 5 minutes, until brown, stirring regularly. Set the mushrooms in aside.

2. Lower the heat to medium and mix 2 more tbsps of butter into the pot. Mix in the onions, garlic, salt and pepper to taste and stir until the onions have softened – about 5 minutes. Add in the beef into the pot and mix

with the onions and spices, breaking the meat apart as you stir. Cook until the meat has browned.

3. Mix in the paprika and flour, stir for another 2 minutes then add in the broth and mustard and mix well. Bring the pot to a medium-high and then lower to a simmer.

4. Bring the mushrooms back into the pot and stir for an additional 3-4 more minutes.

5. Remove from heat and stir the yogurt in. Season again with salt and pepper and garnish with parsley.

6. Serve with your desired carbs, such as pasta, mashed potatoes or rice.

3. Glazed Sticky Pork

This juicy, sweet and tender recipe for preparing pork is a divine combination of garlic, ginger, and sweet, sticky sauce. If you're feeling for a meaty, saucy dish, this will surely satisfy those cravings!

Prep Time: 15 minutes

Cooking Time: 10 minutes

Nutritional Facts/Info:		
4 Servings	Per Serving	

Calories	269	
Carbs	25g	
Fat	6g	
Protein	25g	

Ingredients:

- 1 ½ lbs of pork loin, cut into 3 inch long strips
- 1 tsp of salt
- ½ tsp of pepper
- 1 tbsp of oil
- 3 tbsps of garlic paste
- 2 inches of ginger, grated
- 4 tbsps of sriracha sauce (or more, if you'd like it extra spicy)
- ½ cup of honey
- 1 tbsp of white wine vinegar

Directions:

1. In a small bowl, whisk the honey, sriracha and white wine vinegar together until well mixed, then set aside.
2. Season the pork strips with salt and pepper and toss to fully, evenly coat them.

3. Heat a medium pan over medium-high heat and drizzle the oil to lightly coat the pan. Bring to a simmer and then place in the pork strips – do this in batches so that the strips do not touch one another. Once browned, flip the strips over and fry the other side; it should take 2-3 minutes on either side.

4. Set the pork strips aside and pour the garlic and ginger into the pan, stirring for about 30 seconds. Raise to a high heat and pour the honey mixture into the pan, stirring well to combine. When the sauce begins to boil and thicken, stir the pork strips back into the pan and mix well to evenly coat the strips.

5. You can serve hot or cold.

4. Barbecue Pork Ribs

Pork ribs are always a great option, be it an appetizer or a main meal at a dinner party – the juicy, sticky sauce to meat ratio is undeniably, mouth-wateringly delicious!

Prep Time: 15 minutes

Cooking Time: 2 hours 15 minutes

Nutritional Facts/Info:		
6 Servings	Per Serving	
Calories	814	41%
Carbs	39g	13%
Fat	55g	85%
Protein	38g	76%

Ingredients:

- 4 lbs of pork ribs (2 racks)
- ¾ cup of apple cider
- 1 tbsp of olive oil

Barbecue rub:

- 3 tsps of paprika
- 2 tsps of garlic powder
- 1 ½ tsps of onion powder
- 1 tsp of cayenne pepper
- 1 ½ tsps of thyme
- 1 ½ of oregano
- 1 ½ tsp of salt
- ½ tsp of pepper

Barbecue sauce:

- 1 tsp of salt
- 1 tsp of pepper
- ½ cup of apple cider vinegar
- 1 ½ cups of ketchup
- ½ cup of water
- 1 ½ tbsp molasses
- ⅓ cup of brown sugar
- 2 tsps of mustard powder
- 1 ½ tsp of garlic powder
- 2 tsps of Worcestershire sauce
- 1 tsps of Tabasco

Directions:

1. In a small bowl, mix together all of the ingredients for the barbecue rub and massage well into the pork ribs. Set aside to marinade for at least 20 minutes.
2. When ready to cook, preheat your oven to 350°F and prepare a baking tray. Layer all of the ribs onto the tray and drizzle them with apple cider vinegar (coat underneath the ribs too). Cover the tray with foil and place in the oven for 1 hour and 30 minutes.
3. While the ribs are baking, mix the barbecue sauce in a bowl and set aside.
4. Closer to when the ribs are done, prepare another baking tray by lining with foil and then a layer of

parchment paper over. Remove the ribs from the oven and place on the new tray, generously pouring the leftover juices from the tray over the ribs, coating well.

5. Flip the ribs over so that the boney sides are faced up, and baste the ribs in ¼ of the barbecue sauce. Place back in the oven for another 10 minutes.

6. Remove the ribs from the oven, flip them over and baste in another ¼ of sauce. Bake for another 5 minutes. Repeat this process, baking 5 minutes on each side, until the sauce is finished.

7. Slice the ribs into portions and serve!

5. Stuffed Cabbage Rolls

These sweet and savory cabbage rolls are stuffed with hearty beef and rice mixtures, and topped off by slow-baking in a pot of tomato sauce. Perfect for a weeknight dinner or a family get-together!

Prep Time: 15 minutes

Cooking Time: 45 minutes

Nutritional Facts/Info:		
4 Servings	Per Serving	

Calories	586	
Carbs	57.4g	19.1%
Fat	28.3g	43.5%
Protein	31.1g	62.1%

Ingredients:

For the cabbage & sauce:

- 1 cabbage head
- 1 tbsp of olive oil
- 1 onion, diced
- ¾ tsps of salt
- ¼ black pepper
- 1 can of tomatoes & the tomato juice
- 2 tbsps of apple cider vinegar
- ¼ cup of raisins
- 3 tbsps of brown sugar

For the cabbage filling:

- ⅓ cup of uncooked rice
- 1 large egg
- 1 lb of ground beef
- ¼ cup of diced onion
- ½ tbsp of garlic paste

- 2 tsps of salt
- 1 tsp of paprika
- ¼ tsp of black pepper

Directions:

1. Bring a large pot of water to boil and wash the cabbage. Cut the cabbage in half; remove about 10-12 outer leaves. Place the leaves in the water and boil for about 2 minutes until wilted. Scoop the leaves out using a fork and place on a paper towel to drain.

2. In a large, deep-set pan, heat the oil over medium heat until simmering. Place in the onions and stir for 5 minutes until softened. Then pour in the tomatoes, vinegar, raisins, sugar, salt and pepper and stir well. Leave to simmer for 15 minutes; prepare the cabbage filling in the meanwhile.

3. Combine all the filling ingredients except for the beef, in a bowl and stir well. Slowly stir the beef, and then divide into 8 equal parts. Roll the portions into balls and place the meatballs into the centers of cabbage leaves and then wrap the cabbage around the balls, completely covering the meat mix. Use 2 leaves for meatballs if needed.

4. On a baking sheet, place the cabbage balls with their folds facing down. When the sauce is ready, place the cabbage balls into the pan with their seam-sides facing

downwards. Spoon the sauce over the balls to cover them well. Cover the pot and leave to simmer for 35-40 minutes, until the rice filling is cooked.

Conclusion

With all these homey, delicious homemade recipe options – from spicy Mexican, to In-N-Out Copycat burgers, to Italian pastas and healthy salad options – home cooking is not only easy, but also so fun and so much more budget friendly!

Hopefully these recipes help to comfort all your possible fast food cravings, and that you find a few new recipes that you'll use quite often in the future! It's also important to remember: all of these recipes can be altered/experimented with, to comfort your taste. Slay these recipes, and make them yours!

These are stepping stones for you to master and make these recipes your own by adding your own style and twist on these dishes, and most importantly: have fun!

Did you enjoy this book? Please let me know your thoughts by leaving a short review on Amazon. Thanks again.

References

8 Quick and Easy Pasta Recipes | RecipeTin Eats.
https://www.recipetineats.com/

19 Perfect Pasta Dishes You'll Want to Make for Dinner
Tonight. Real Simple.
https://www.realsimple.com/food-recipes/recipe-
collections-favorites/popular-ingredients/pasta-
recipes?slide=5aeaf6d8-5ac8-4aaf-a179-
e67e204423b9

Bauer, E. The Best Lasagna Recipe {Simple & Classic}.
Simply Recipes.
https://www.simplyrecipes.com/recipes/lasagna/

Bauer, E. (2020, May 30). How to Make Eggs Benedict
Recipe.
https://www.simplyrecipes.com/recipes/eggs_benedi
ct/

Cauliflower Pizza Crust. Food Network.
https://www.foodnetwork.com/recipes/katie-
lee/cauliflower-pizza-crust-2651381

Cauliflower Risotto With Mushrooms. Cooking Light.
https://www.cookinglight.com/recipes/cauliflower-
risotto

Chef Laurel Hudson. Vanilla French Toast Dunkers.
BigOven.com.
https://www.bigoven.com/recipe/vanilla-french-
toast-dunkers/180983

Chick, T. A. (2020, May 28). Simple Seafood Appetizers
Recipe. Yummly.

https://www.yummly.com/recipe/Simple-Seafood-Appetizers-1278579.

Detroit-Style Pepperoni Pizza. Food Network. https://www.foodnetwork.com/recipes/jeff-mauro/detroit-style-pepperoni-pizza-4718298

Diethood, K. |. (2020, February 26). Olive Garden's Zuppa Toscana: Easy Olive Garden Copycat Recipe. Diethood. https://diethood.com/gnocchi-zuppa-toscana-recipe/.

Eidelstein, A. (2018, May 10). Lemony Cucumber-and-Herb Pasta Salad. Real Simple. https://www.realsimple.com/food-recipes/browse-all-recipes/lemony-cucumber-herb-pasta-salad

Elick, D. (1970, January 1). Wendy's Chili Copycat (With Video). The Slow Roasted Italian. https://www.theslowroasteditalian.com/2014/01/wendys-chili-copycat-recipe.html

Fountaine, S., Sandy, David, Lou, Terry, T., J., ... Welch, N. (2020, January 8). Mushroom Wellington with Rosemary and Pecans. Feasting At Home. https://www.feastingathome.com/mushroom-wellington-rosemary-pecans/

Fountaine, S., Mona, Katie, Alfeo, B., Hailey, & Pammy. (2019, November 14). Warm Lentils with Wilted Chard, Roasted Beets and Goat Cheese. Feasting At Home. https://www.feastingathome.com/warm-lentils-wilted-chard-roasted-beets-and-goat-cheese/

Fountaine, S., Taruc, G., Andraski, L., Ola, Alex, Kelsey, ... Theresa. (2020, May 30). Palak Paneer (Paneer in

Fragrant Spinach Sauce). Feasting At Home. https://www.feastingathome.com/palak-paneer/

Fuhr, L. (2016, April 24). DIY Starbucks Spinach-Feta Wrap. POPSUGAR Fitness. https://www.popsugar.com/fitness/Starbucks-Spinach-Feta-Wrap-Recipe-31666375?utm_campaign=default_hp

Gallary, C. (2019, November 7). Recipe: One-Pot Weeknight Beef Stroganoff. Kitchn. https://www.thekitchn.com/recipe-one-pot-weeknight-beef-stroganoff-249761

Gallary, C. (2019, May 1). Recipe: Weeknight Cabbage Rolls. Kitchn. https://www.thekitchn.com/recipe-weeknight-cabbage-rolls-239430

Gore, M. (2020, January 3). A Deep Dish Pizza Better Than Chicago Could Make. Delish. https://www.delish.com/cooking/recipe-ideas/a25561571/deep-dish-pizza-recipe/

Grandjean, P. (2017, February 27). Roasted Eggplant and Olive Pasta Salad. Real Simple. https://www.realsimple.com/food-recipes/browse-all-recipes/roasted-eggplant-olive-pasta-salad

Grandjean, P. (2018, March 8). Wild Mushroom and Spinach Stuffed Shells. Real Simple. https://www.realsimple.com/food-recipes/browse-all-recipes/wild-mushroom-spinach-stuffed-shells.

Grandjean, P. (2018, March 8). Pasta, Chickpea, and Chicken Soup With Pesto. Real Simple.

https://www.realsimple.com/food-recipes/browse-all-recipes/pasta-chickpea-chicken-soup-pesto.

Greek Meatballs - healthy & gluten-free. Rachel Cooks®. (2020, March 2). https://www.rachelcooks.com/2017/08/28/greek-meatballs/.

Hackett, D., Freeman, B., Guzman, P. P., & B., K. (2020, March 29). Easy Homemade Pizza Sauce Recipe (5- Minutes)! JoyFoodSunshine. https://joyfoodsunshine.com/easy-homemade-pizza-sauce-recipe/

Healthy Breakfast Smoothies - 21 Quick & Easy Recipes. (2019, December 19). https://kristineskitchenblog.com/21-healthy-breakfast-smoothie-recipes/

Hilina, Louise, Stacey, H, L., Josh, Kelsey, ... Bethany @ Athletic Avocado. (2020, March 18). Quick & Easy Creamy Herb Chicken. Cafe Delites. https://cafedelites.com/quick-easy-creamy-herb-chicken/

Homemade Crunchwrap Supreme. Bless This Food. http://blessthisfood.blogspot.com/2012/01/homemade-crunchwrap-supreme.html

Homemade Pizza Crust for Beginners | Sally's Baking Addiction. https://sallysbakingaddiction.com/homemade-pizza-crust-recipe/

Homemade Sushi Recipe - Surprisingly Easy To Make Yourself. Fifteen Spatulas. (2019, September 18). https://www.fifteenspatulas.com/homemade-sushi/

Indian Appetizer Recipes. The Spruce Eats. https://www.thespruceeats.com/indian-appetizers-4162608.

JamieOliver.com. (2020, January 27). How to make French toast: Features. https://www.jamieoliver.com/features/how-to-make-french-toast/

Julia, Jenn, & Cedar Spoon. (2017, December 19). 15 Must Make Mediterranean Appetizers. A Cedar Spoon. https://www.acedarspoon.com/15-must-make-mediterranean-appetizers/.

Kenna, J. (2017, April 26). Cozy Chicken And Dumplings Recipe by Tasty. tasty.co. https://tasty.co/recipe/cozy-chicken-and-dumplings

Kennedy, E., Mozo, B., Biñas, G., Faythe, Hillary, & Crystal. (2014, July 28). Copycat Krispy Kreme Recipe for National Doughnut Day. MyThirtySpot. https://www.mythirtyspot.com/krispy-kreme-copycat-recipe-for/

Kitchens, B. C. (2008, September 30). Creamy Seafood Pasta. BettyCrocker.com. https://www.bettycrocker.com/recipes/creamy-seafood-pasta/c6baa90b-3509-408a-aeae-f0021905eff0

Killebrew, K., Hanna, C., Carol, Pearlyn, VeniceParrish, Allen, A., ... Wood, S. (2020, April 10). Easy Homemade Tahini. The Daring Gourmet. https://www.daringgourmet.com/how-to-make-homemade-tahini-paste/

Kitchens, B. C. (2016, February 10). Italian Stuffed Mushrooms. BettyCrocker.com. https://www.bettycrocker.com/recipes/italian-stuffed-mushrooms/4a4953fb-a28d-4c5e-b30a-8b37b6d54e8b.

Layla. (2020, May 28). Easy 20 Minute Butter Chicken. Gimme Delicious. https://gimmedelicious.com/easy-20-minute-butter-chicken/

Leah, Crystelle, Liz, Marista, Cedar Spoon, Lightened Chicken Salad, ... Mediterranean Eggplant Salad - A Cedar Spoon. (2019, August 1). Eggplant Dip {Baba Ghanoush} Recipe. A Cedar Spoon. https://www.acedarspoon.com/eggplant-dip-baba-ghanoush/.

Lindsay, Helen, Jodie, Alyson, Jerome, Kristin, . . . Emily @ Zen & Spice. (2020, May 01). Simple Poached Egg and Avocado Toast. https://pinchofyum.com/simple-poached-egg-avocado-toast

Lindsay, Jakky, Jenna, Kelli, Rosanna, Spivey, D., ... Cs. (2020, April 30). Life-Changing Crispy Fried Pizzas. Pinch of Yum. https://pinchofyum.com/life-changing-fried-pizzas

López-Alt, J. K. New York-Style Pizza Recipe. Serious Eats. https://www.seriouseats.com/recipes/2010/10/new-york-style-pizza.html.

López-Alt, J. K., Russock, C., Gritzer, D., Instagram, & Facebook. A Better Big Mac Recipe. Serious Eats. https://www.seriouseats.com/recipes/2011/05/a-better-big-mac-mcdonalds-burger-recipe.html

López-Alt, J. K., Russock, C., Instagram, & Facebook. The Fake Shack, Mach Two: The Double Shack Stack Cracked Recipe. Serious Eats. https://www.seriouseats.com/recipes/2011/01/the-fake-shack-mach-two-double-shack-stack-burger-recipe.html

López-Alt, J. K., Russock, C., Chin, T., Gritzer, D., Instagram, & Facebook. In-N-Out's Double-Double, Animal Style Recipe. Serious Eats. https://www.seriouseats.com/recipes/2010/07/in-n-outs-double-double-animal-style-burger-recipe.html

López-Alt, J. K., Russock, C., Instagram, & Facebook. Takeout-Style Kung Pao Chicken (Diced Chicken With Peppers and Peanuts) Recipe. Serious Eats. https://www.seriouseats.com/recipes/2014/07/takeout-style-kung-pao-chicken-diced-chicken-peppers-peanuts-recipe.html

Lu, Marielena, King, D., Mary, Anne, Catia, … Two Peas. (2020, April 9). Caprese Garlic Bread Recipe. Two Peas & Their Pod. https://www.twopeasandtheirpod.com/caprese-garlic-bread/?m.

Mesquita, O., Regina, Krysten, Diana, Aish, Shelley, . . . Oswald. (2019, July 12). New York-Style Bacon Egg and Cheese. https://www.oliviascuisine.com/new-york-style-bacon-egg-and-cheese/

Morin, C. (2019, September 11). Learn How to Make a Tasty Authentic Jamaican Jerk Sauce at Home. The Spruce Eats. https://www.thespruceeats.com/jamaican-jerk-sauce-recipe-1806844

Nagi, Christie, Tina, Steveshooman, Bethany, Davis, N., & Lindow, T. (2020, January 16). Truly Crispy Oven Baked Chicken Tenders. RecipeTin Eats. https://www.recipetineats.com/truly-golden-crunchy-baked-chicken-tenders-less-mess/

Nagi, Leanne, Nada, Mazzoni, L., Kate, Philip, & Martin. (2020, February 15). Oven Pork Ribs with Barbecue Sauce. RecipeTin Eats. https://www.recipetineats.com/oven-baked-barbecue-pork-ribs/

Nagi, Shields, D., Janel, Kathleen, Rajesh, Yj, ... Steve. (2020, March 4). Oven Baked Tandoori Chicken. RecipeTin Eats. https://www.recipetineats.com/oven-baked-tandoori-chicken/

Nagi, Verna, Chris, Fredrickson, P., & Jacqueline. (2019, October 8). Emergency EASY Fish recipe - Parmesan Crumbed Fish! RecipeTin Eats. https://www.recipetineats.com/healthy-parmesan-garlic-crumbed-fish/

NDTV Food. (2014, July 21). Mexican Barbeque Sauce Recipe by Niru Gupta. NDTV Food. https://food.ndtv.com/recipe-mexican-barbeque-sauce-2-562207

Nicole, Baker, Dana, Sorcha, Charon, Hannah, ... Paridhi. (2020, April 22). How to Make Sushi at Home: Minimalist Baker Recipes. Minimalist Baker. https://minimalistbaker.com/how-to-make-sushi-without-a-mat/

Olena. (2019, October 18). 35 Quick and Easy Healthy Breakfast Ideas - iFOODreal - Healthy Family Recipes. https://ifoodreal.com/breakfast-meal-prep/

Olga, & Fablunch. (2017, August 20). 5 Must-Try Smoothie Bowls. https://blog.fablunch.com/5-must-try-smoothie-bowls/

Parsons, B. C., Barb, Emilie, Irene, Kevin, Coffin, B., ... Louise. (2020, May 9). Copycat KFC? Is the leaked recipe the real deal? Rock Recipes. https://www.rockrecipes.com/copycat-kfc/

Person. (2018, March 22). Primavera Skillet Pizza. Delish. https://www.delish.com/cooking/recipe-ideas/recipes/a46837/primavera-skillet-pizza-recipe/

Rattray, D. (2019, August 29). Add Zest to Your Fish or Seafood With This Tangy Remoulade Sauce. The Spruce Eats. https://www.thespruceeats.com/basic-remoulade-sauce-3060568

Rattray, D. (2019, August 30). Try This Tasty Recipe for an Easy Caramel Dessert Sauce. The Spruce Eats. https://www.thespruceeats.com/easy-caramel-sauce-recipe-3051812

Rebecca, Lindamood, R., Melissa, Rie, Robby, Wiegand, A., ... Slow Cooker Five Spice Pork Ramen. (2020, February 3). Easy Garlic Ginger Glazed Sticky Pork. Foodie With Family. https://www.foodiewithfamily.com/easy-garlic-ginger-glazed-sticky-pork/

Rhee, C. (2018, August 28). Shrimp Scampi Gnocchi. Damn Delicious. https://damndelicious.net/2018/08/26/shrimp-scampi-gnocchi/

Rhee, C. (2019, October 18). Easy Clam Chowder. Damn Delicious.

https://damndelicious.net/2015/04/25/easy-clam-chowder/

Rattray, D. (2019, August 30). Try This Tasty Recipe for an Easy Caramel Dessert Sauce. The Spruce Eats. https://www.thespruceeats.com/easy-caramel-sauce-recipe-3051812

Sage, H. (2020, May 22). 21 One-Bite Appetizer Recipe Ideas for Your Big Game Party. Brit + Co. https://www.brit.co/bite-size-super-bowl-appetizers/.

Samina, Eileen, Sillabe, Jocelyn, Anna, Abbi, ... American Heritage Cooking. Cheesy Ravioli and Italian Sausage Skillet. The Comfort of Cooking. http://www.thecomfortofcooking.com/2014/06/cheesy-ravioli-and-italian-sausage-skillet.html

Schmidt, D. (2019, May 20). Traditional Thai Satay Peanut Sauce With Real Peanuts. The Spruce Eats. https://www.thespruceeats.com/thai-peanut-sauce-marinade-noodles-salad-3217705

Shelley, Arturo, Lang, Debi, Two Healthy Kitchens, & Life Currents. (2018, July 22). 9 All-Time Best Healthy, Easy Seafood and Fish Recipes. Two Healthy Kitchens. https://twohealthykitchens.com/9-all-time-best-healthy-easy-seafood-and-fish-recipes/

Shihoko, McDoogle, D., Jaycee, Pua, Rani, Elzi, F., ... Dorothy. (2019, June 17). Tempura - how to cook crispy tempura 天ぷら. Chopstick Chronicles. https://www.chopstickchronicles.com/tempura/

Simmons, M., Katie, 1., Donofrio, J., Cheryl, 1., Dalkin, G., Jamie, . . . Akhil. (2020, January 27). How to Make a

Frittata Recipe.
https://www.loveandlemons.com/frittata-recipe/

Simon, S. (2020, May 06). 20 Breakfast Bowl Recipes to
Jump-Start Your Morning.
https://www.brit.co/breakfast-bowls/

Splawn, M. (2019, November 18). How To Cook Perfect
Steak on the Stovetop in 3 Steps. Kitchn.
https://www.thekitchn.com/how-to-cook-steak-on-
the-stovetop-240330

St.Louis Style Pizza (Imo's Copy Cat). Cooking for Keeps.
(2019, August 28).
https://www.cookingforkeeps.com/copycat-imos-st-
louis-style-pizza-yeast-rest-crust/

Sweet Appetizers Recipes. Yummly.
https://www.yummly.com/recipes/sweet-appetizers.

The Best Chicken Soup You'll Ever Eat. Ambitious Kitchen.
(2020, January 6).
https://www.ambitiouskitchen.com/the-best-
chicken-soup-recipe/

Trish, McAlpine, L., Deborah, Kerry, Brady, L., Melanie, ...
Michelle. (2019, May 21). Easy Chicken Stir Fry
Recipe. Mom On Timeout.
https://www.momontimeout.com/easy-chicken-stir-
fry-recipe/

Uptergrove, S., Chris, Marie, R., Carolann, Janine, Sam, ...
Vanessa. (2020, May 24). 25 BEST Appetizers to
Serve for Holiday Party Entertaining! A Blissful Nest.
https://ablissfulnest.com/best-appetizers-to-serve/.

Valley, C. (2019, May 10). 30 Easy Appetizers. Family Fresh Meals. https://www.familyfreshmeals.com/2014/12/30-easy-appetizers-people-love.html.

World's Best Pasta Sauce! Allrecipes. https://www.allrecipes.com/recipe/130358/worlds-best-pasta-sauce/

Keto Copycat Recipes

An Easy Step-by-Step Guide for Making Your Favorite Tasty Keto Restaurant's Dishes at Home, With Healthy Recipes to Lose Weight on the Ketogenic Diet

Lisa Ramsey

Introduction

Dieting is a struggle for many. When one begins a diet, there is a lot of emphasis on what you can't have, which automatically sets you up for failure. When you have to keep reminding yourself what you aren't allowed to consume it just makes you want those things even more. Going out to eat becomes a frustrating occurrence as you look over the menu and begin checking off all the items you can't order because of your diet.

Those on the keto diet know this scenario all too well. Your favorite menu items are now off limits. You can't conveniently drive up to a drive-thru and order something quick while you are rushing to work or stop by to pick up an order from your favorite restaurant. You avoid going out to eat because sitting down just to order a salad, when you probably can't even have the dressing, isn't as much fun as ordering the steak and potatoes. I remember when I first decided to start on the keto diet. It was a struggle to cut out the carbs and replace them with keto-friendly alternatives. I was clueless about how to make meals and found myself starting and stopping with no success.

After many failed attempts I was about to give up. I wasn't kitchen savvy at the time, and the whole idea of trying to figure out what I could actually cook with was overwhelming, and I would quickly grow tired of the same old broiled chicken and steamed veggies. What was even more discouraging is I missed those fast-food burgers and sweet treats. But the Keto diet doesn't have to be and should not be all bland foods and salads.

After a great deal of researching and experimenting, I was able to successfully understand how I could recreate my favorite restaurant foods from the convenience of my own kitchen! This book is designed to give you this understanding. So, you don't have to suffer through boring meals and failed attempts on the keto diet.

While there are guidelines to follow, the keto diet focuses on what you can eat. It encourages you to consume more healthy fats, proteins, and vegetables while also keeping an eye on your carbohydrate intake. It can help you lose weight, improve your heart health, regulate your digestive tract, increase your energy, and so much more.

You don't have to count calories, restrict your portion sizes, or deprive yourself of the foods you love! You can still enjoy your burgers, comfort foods, and even dessert. You just have to learn how to make this diet work for you and be open minded about trying new foods and ingredients.

This book is designed to show you how easy it is to create mouthwatering keto recipes in your own home. You will find recipes from some of the most well-known fast-food places and chain restaurants that cover breakfast, lunch, dinner, and yes, even desserts! What is even better, these recipes not only taste just like what you would typically order, but many taste even better.

Whether you have been on the keto diet for a while and need some more recipes ideas, or you are just starting out, you will find the recipes in this book refreshing and enjoyable. Additionally, all the recipes are super simple to create. You don't need to have any kitchen skills to successfully recreate these meals. You don't have to focus on what you can't have while on the keto diet when you have an arsenal of delicious recipes to try. You will find that just about any meal you used to love, you can still enjoy when you swap in keto-friendly ingredients, which can be easily found at your local grocery store or conveniently ordered online.

If you are tired of not seeing the result you desire while on the keto diet, don't want to feel like your diet is so restrictive, and want to create delicious meals that excite you, then all you have to do is turn the page!

So read this book now and don't forget to let me know what you think with a short review if you enjoy it. Thanks!

Chapter 1: What Is Keto?

The keto diet has gained in popularity over recent years. It has been touted as a quick way to lose weight and improve overall health. While many people have had success on this diet, a greater number have found it ineffective or have had success only to see the weight immediately come back when they stop the diet. There are a number of reasons why you may be considering this diet or may have started but are discouraged because you haven't seen the weight fall off as you had hoped. This chapter will provide you with the general information you need to know to understand exactly how this diet works and how to make it work for you. First, you will understand why cutting back on carbs can promote weight loss; then you will learn what steps to take so you don't have to fail over and over again when trying to lose weight.

The Ketogenic Diet

The ketogenic diet is a high-fat, low-carb diet that is similar to the popular Atkins diet and other low-carb meal plans. On this diet, you swap out carbs and replace them with fats for the most part. It sounds simple enough, but many people think that means they can eat all the bacon they want and enjoy a number of food items that may be low carb but are actually not beneficial to your health. This is the number one reason why many people fail to see the result they desire when starting a keto diet.

The goal of this diet is to shift the body into a natural state of ketosis where the body uses ketones as its main source of fuel as opposed to glucose. Ketosis is achieved when your body begins to use up the fat stored in the body for fuel over the expectation of being fueled through glucose. Glucose is formed from the carbohydrates you consume, specifically simple carbs like sugars and complex carbohydrates like white flours, pasta, grains, and rice. To kick start ketosis, one must drastically reduce the carbs they consume that will be absorbed by the body and increase the healthy fats to supply it with sufficient fuel.

The transition can take up to two weeks to finally occur if you consistently stick to the diet guidelines. Where many people go wrong with this diet is that they stick to the food recommendations for a few days, then have a little "cheat" meal or treat and don't realize they now have to start back at day one. Most people are also simply unaware of how many items they consume that are loaded with hidden sugars and grains.

This is what can make the keto diet challenging. It takes your full commitment, and when individuals hear that, they shrink away. In reality, it is not that difficult to make the switch to this type of diet, but it does take a little more effort at the beginning and more awareness of what you are eating.

Variations of the Keto Diet

1. Targeted keto diet - This type of keto diet is favored by a number of professional athletes. It helps you time when to eat the right carbs at the right time in relation to when you are working out. When you fuel your body in this way, your body learns to quickly use the carbs as fuel in the most efficient way to help you increase your endurance and performance when working out. This type of keto diet is especially beneficial for those who are trying to build more muscles or who are trying to maintain muscle mass.

2. Cyclical keto diet - The cyclical keto diet incorporates what is referred to as refeed days. With this diet plan, you will schedule in days where you slightly increase your carbs and even allow yourself to have what are considered not-as-good-for-you carbs like white flours, pasta, or natural sugars. What this does is provide your body with a slight boost in glucose which provides your body with additional fuel that can help it burn more fat. Typically, you would follow a stricter keto diet plan for five days then allow yourself two refeed days. This, however, is meant to be an additional plan you follow

after you have successfully stuck to a standard keto plan. It is also highly recommended that you include regular exercise in your new lifestyle as the exercises are what trigger the body to burn through more of its stored fuel.

3. Standard keto diet - When you hear about the keto diet, it is most likely that people are referring to the standard keto diet. With this approach, your diet consists of a moderate amount of protein and fat with minimal carbs. The standard keto diet consists of 5% of your foods being carbs, 75% of your foods are healthy fats, and the remaining 20% of the food you consume will be proteins. Many individuals find it easier to transition to a standard keto diet and then move into another type of keto diet or incorporate another keto diet into their lifestyle.

4. High-protein keto diet - This is very similar to the standard keto diet. The only difference between the two is that with the high-protein keto diet, your protein will make up 35% of what you eat ,and healthy fats will make up 60% of what you eat. The carb intake remains the same at 5%.

What makes this diet more appealing than most other diets is that you don't have to count calories or restrict the number of calories you consume.

What to Eat?

Seafood: Fatty fish like salmon, tuna, and sardines are encouraged on the keto diet. Not only do they provide you with lean protein, they contain omega-3s that help promote brain and heart health.

Cheese: While a number of dairy products are off limits, cheese is not one of them. Unprocessed cheese such as mozzarella, cheddar, bleu cheese, and cream cheese can be eaten freely. Cheese contains a healthy amount of fats and provides the body with the necessary calcium to strengthen bones.

Avocado: Avocados contain a high amount of fat, which is why they are recommended to only be consumed in moderation on most other diets. The fats in avocado, however, are healthy fats that can benefit the body. On the keto diet, avocado is used in a number of ways, from creating spreads for breadless sandwiches to using the oil for cooking.

Red Meat: All types of red meats are approved on the keto diet. Keep in mind lean meat and grass-fed meats are favored over processed meats like prepackaged deli meats or processed meats.

Poultry: Chicken and turkey are also allowed on the keto diet with no restriction. Again, choosing free-range poultry is encouraged.

Eggs: Eggs contain protein and healthy fats and are a regular staple of the keto diet.

Nonstarchy vegetables: Vegetables can be consumed freely on the keto diet, except for starchy vegetables, like potatoes. You can literally eat as many dark leafy greens and a wide variety of vegetables as you want throughout the day. Since most vegetables contain little-to-no carbs and they also have a low caloric index, eating more vegetables can promote weight loss.

Nuts and seeds: Nuts and seeds can provide you with a good source of healthy fats. They are often added to a number of keto dishes and can be eaten as a snack throughout the day while on the keto diet.

Berries: Most fruits are excluded from the keto diet, but berries like strawberries, blackberries, and raspberries are allowed in low quantities. Blueberries are also OK, but they do have a slightly higher carb level than other berries, so you will need to carefully watch how many you consume.

Herbs and spices: Herb and spices of all varieties are used in keto meals to not only add more flavor but to accommodate for certain ingredients that you would typically find in a recipe but are avoiding while on the keto diet. You will notice the recipes in this book have plenty of spices and herbs on the ingredient list, even the desserts. This is so you get the same flavor from your meals as you would if you were not on the keto diet. Spices and herbs are what can really help you stick with the keto diet as they keep your meals interesting and enticing.

What to Avoid?

The keto diet focuses on reducing the number of carbs you take in. Specifically, it is the carbs that are absorbed by the body that you want to reduce. These carbs, such as those consumed when we eat processed sugars or wheat products, increase glucose levels in the body. If there is an excess amount of glucose in the body, it gets stored away as fat, which is what we are trying to eliminate. This means there are a number of food items you want to avoid and cut out completely when you are on the keto diet.

These items include:

Sugars: This includes sugar drinks like pop, fruit juices, and teas as well as food items like prepackaged snack cakes, candy, ice cream, and processed foods. A majority of prepackaged foods you find on the grocery store shelves contain added sugar, so you will need to learn to carefully look at the ingredient list to identify where these sugar culprits are being snuck in.

Grains and starches: Even grains that are considered healthy like quinoa, whole wheat, or whole grain are avoided when on the keto diet. This is because these starches are converted into glucose once processed by the body.

Beans and legumes: Though a number of beans and legumes provide a variety of vitamins and nutrients, they too are processed and converted into glucose.

Root vegetables: Potatoes and sweet potatoes are starchy vegetables. They contain a high amount of carbohydrates, which is why when you are on the keto diet, these types of vegetables are omitted from meal plans.

Fruits: This is where the keto diet gets a lot of criticism. While most fruits do offer a wide array of beneficial vitamins and nutrients, they are also loaded with a significant amount of sugar. Even though these are natural sugars and considered better for you, they still spike glucose levels and promote storing fat in the body.

Getting Started

If you want to have success with the keto diet, you can begin to take a few steps that will improve your chances of reaching your weight loss goals and really making this diet a long-term lifestyle. Even if you decide that the keto diet isn't for you, the following steps can help you better understand your eating habits and identify where you can make changes to improve your overall health.

Step 1 - Tracking

One of the first things you want to do before you even get started on the keto diet is to begin tracking what you eat and when. This is important because in order to know what changes to your diet you need to make, you need to understand and be honest about what your diet is like now. When tracking, you want to write down everything you consume, both foods and drinks. Write when you eat, how much you ate, and also take note of any emotion you may be feeling. Emotional eating is a real struggle for many to overcome. By making a little note of when you may be eating because of stress, boredom, sadness, or even when you are happy, you can recognize that these are times when you can turn to different and more beneficial coping mechanisms instead of food.

You will want to track what you eat for at least two weeks. By doing this, you can begin to identify patterns to your eating habits and create a plan for how to transition to a keto diet. Even after the first week of tracking, you can begin to implement more keto-friendly foods into your diet to make the transition seamless and easier.

Step 2 - Make small changes.

After you have been tracking what you eat for two weeks, begin to make small changes to your diet. Swap out high-carbs snacks for nuts, seeds, or vegetables. Begin to experiment with more keto-friendly ingredients when you cook, like using different sweeteners or substituting in almond flour, coconut flour, or flaxseed for all-purpose flour. Making small changes is less overwhelming than trying to change everything overnight.

See where you can easily add in more proteins and healthy fats. You will want to begin cutting back on those items you will eventually eliminate from your diet. Sugary drinks are often one of the easiest and most common items that people begin to swap out. Instead of pop, juices, or stopping by your local coffee house for a fancy coffee, drink more water or seltzer and make coffee at home without the added sugars and creamers.

Take it one step at a time. It isn't a race and making one small change each week will often lead to more success in the long run.

Step 3 - Change the way you shop.

When you commit to a keto diet, you will find that going to the grocery store can be a real challenge. A number of products have high amounts of sugars and hidden carbs that will throw you off your meal plan. Begin to understand how to read food labels and how to calculate your net carbs. This will allow you to make better choices when you are shopping and know what you should avoid. When you do go grocery shopping, stick to the perimeter of the store and avoid the middle aisles. Most of the foods on the shelves you're not going to want to buy, but the outer aisles tend to have your fresh produce and lean meats, which is where you will want to get a majority of your food.

Step 4 - Commit.

The keto diet isn't something that you can do once in a while. For your body to enter into its natural state of ketosis, you need to be consistent every single day. Don't let that intimidate you though. Once you get used to swapping out certain foods, the keto diet simply becomes your new way of eating. When you are just beginning, however, it is crucial that you stick with a low-carb meal plan. If you try to sneak in a cheat meal, you can be knocked out of ketosis, and the process will need to begin all over again.

What to Keep in Mind

Before beginning on any new diet, you want to consult with your doctor first. Since the keto diet does restrict carbs, this may not be beneficial for all types of people. It is better to check in with your doctor and go over any health concerns you may have that can make sticking to this diet more of a challenge. Those with diabetes especially should go over your current health before beginning the keto diet. Though the keto diet can help regulate insulin levels and lower glucose level, people with diabetes are at a higher risk developing hypoglycemia, where the blood pressure drops too low, and ketoacidosis. Ketoacidosis occurs when too many ketones build up in the body, which can cause serious health complications. If you have diabetes, you will want to learn how to check your ketone levels to avoid this risk.

Also, the keto diet is not effective for everyone, but those who stick to it consistently will often have more success. Those looking to lose weight on the keto diet should also add a regular exercise routine to their daily activities. Just as you start slow and make small changes with what you eat on the keto diet, you can begin to take this approach to exercise as well. Your diet is only half of the equation if you want to lose weight. You need to be active in order to reach your weight loss goals. Simply add in 10 minutes of cardio a few times a week. When you make this a habit, increase the amount of time you exercise for or add on another day of exercise.

You want to also be aware that when your body makes the transition into ketosis there can be some uncomfortable side effects. Many individuals have stated that they get flu-like symptoms after they have stuck with the diet for a number of weeks. This can include feeling nauseated, having a slight fever, feeling a drop in energy levels, and muscle pains. These symptoms tend to only last a few days, but when they occur, it can be easy to slip up with your eating habits.

Finally, keep in mind that while your main goal for starting the keto diet is to lose weight, you want to think about the more long-term benefits. Adopting better eating habits and a regular exercise routine should become a new way of living. If you quickly go back to your old eating habits after you have reached your goal weight, you will see the weight pile back on. This will make losing the weight again more difficult.

Now that you have a better understanding of how to approach the keto diet, it is time to supply you with some tools for success. The remainder of this book includes a number of keto recipes that are inspired by and copy some of the most popular fast-food and chain restaurant menu items. These recipes will show you that the keto diet doesn't have to be complex or limiting. You can still enjoy delicious, flavorful meals while losing weight. The recipes that follow all have a brief introduction that provides additional tips, personal stories, and suggestions to help you on your keto diet journey.

Chapter 2: Breakfast

When you are trying to lose weight, breakfast is essential. But busy mornings make it so easy to skip this important meal or even more easy to reach for something that is loaded with sugar and carbs. This chapter will introduce you to a number of those grab-and-go breakfasts that you'd usually stop on your way to work to get but without the excess sugar and abundant carbs.

Starbucks Everything Bagel

Many think that making bagels is a complex process, but this recipe makes it easy, quick, and healthy. You can easily make this recipe your own by using any number of herbs or spices.

Serving Size: 1 bagel

Prep Time: 10 minutes

Cook Time: 12 minutes

Nutritional Information:

Calories 160

Carbs 3 g

Fat 12.5 g

Protein 9 g

Ingredients:

- 2 cups almond flour
- 3 cups mozzarella cheese (shredded)
- 3 eggs
- 5 tablespoons cream cheese
- 3 tablespoons everything bagel seasoning
- 1 teaspoon Italian seasoning
- 1 teaspoon baking powder
- 1 teaspoon garlic powder
- 1 teaspoon onion powder

Directions:

1. Begin by preheating your oven to 425 degrees Fahrenheit, then line a baking sheet with parchment paper.
2. Take a medium-sized mixing bowl and combine the almond flour, garlic powder, onion powder, baking soda, and Italian seasoning. Stir everything together until well incorporated, then set to the side.
3. Take a larger microwave-safe mixing bowl and combine the cream cheese and mozzarella cheese. Place the bowl in the microwave for a minute and a half. Remove from the microwave and stir the cheeses together. Place the bowl back in the microwave and

microwave for another minute. Stir again and repeat until the cheeses are mixed together thoroughly.

4. Add the flour mixture into the bowl with the cheese mixture. Crack two of the eggs into the mixture as well. Stir everything together until you have a soft dough. If the mixture appears to string, then place the bowl back into the microwave for 30 seconds, then mix again.

5. Once you have a soft dough, divide it into 6 equal portions. Roll each portion out into a short tube, then connect the ends so you have a bagel shape. Place each bagel onto your baking sheet.

6. Take the remaining egg and crack it into a small mixing bowl. Use a fork to beat the egg, then use a baking brush to brush the egg on top of each of your bagel shapes.

7. Sprinkle a little of everything bagel seasoning on top of each bagel. Then place the baking sheet into the oven and bake for 12 minutes. The tops of the bagels should be a nice golden-brown color.

8. Remove from the oven and enjoy!

IHop Bacon Temptation Omelet

This is the ultimate protein-packed breakfast. Simply making the swap of whole milk for heavy cream turns this into a keto breakfast you can enjoy!

Serving Size: 1 omelet

Prep Time: 5 minutes

Cook Time: 15 minutes

Nutritional Information:

Calories 878

Carbs 5g

Fat 89g

Protein 64g

Ingredients:

- 4 eggs
- 6 slices of bacon (cooked, cut into pieces)
- ¼ cup Monterey Jack cheese
- ¼ cup cheddar cheese (shredded)
- 2 tablespoons heavy cream

Directions:

1. Place a large skillet on your stove and turn the temperature to medium heat to let the skillet get nice and hot. Place a small pot/saucepan on the stove as well, turn the heat to medium.

2. In the small saucepan, add the cheddar cheese and 1 tablespoon of heavy cream. Stir continuously until the

mixture is smooth, then lower the heat and stir until the sauce begins to thicken slightly.

3. As the sauce is simmering on low heat, take a medium-sized mixing bowl and crack the four eggs into it. Beat the eggs with a fork and add in the remaining tablespoon of heavy cream as well as half the cooked bacon pieces.

4. Pour your egg mixture into your preheated skillet, lower the temperature to medium low, and allow to cook for 3 minutes. Once the eggs have firmed up a bit, take your cheese sauce and pour it over half of the eggs. Sprinkle some of the bacon pieces on top of the cheese sauce (leave a small amount of the bacon pieces to top the omelet with). Top the bacon pieces with half the Monterey Jack cheese.

5. Carefully fold the half of the eggs over on top of the cheese and bacon so that you have a half-moon egg shape in your skillet. Let it cook for another minute so the Monterey Jack cheese begins to melt.

6. Turn the heat off and transfer your omelet to a plate. Top the omelet with the remaining bacon and Monterey Jack cheese.

McDonald's McGriddle Bacon Sandwich

The sweet and salty combination of a McGriddle is nicely replicated in this recipe. You can easily make one batch and have breakfast planned out for the week. The best thing about this recipe? You won't have to wait in a drive-thru line to get one.

Serving Size: 1 sandwich

Prep Time: 10 minutes

Cook Time: 25 minutes

Nutritional Information:

Calories 279

Carbs 1g

Fat 22g

Protein 20g

Ingredients:

- 6 bacon slices
- 6 eggs
- 6 slices cheddar cheese
- ½ teaspoon Himalayan sea salt
- ½ teaspoon black pepper

For the Buns:

- 3 eggs
- 1 cup almond flour
- 2 teaspoons baking powder
- 1 ½ teaspoon erythritol (sweetener)
- ½ teaspoon liquid stevia
- 1 ½ teaspoon vanilla extract
- 1 teaspoon maple extract
- 3 ounces cream cheese

Directions:

1. Begin by preheating the oven to 350 degrees Fahrenheit.

2. As the oven preheats, prepare the buns by combining the eggs, almond flour, baking powder, erythritol, liquid stevia, vanilla extract, maple extract, and cream cheese in a blender. Pulse the ingredients for about 2 minutes until you have a smooth texture.

3. Next, you will need 12 mason jar lids or a whoopie pie pan. Take a baking sheet and line it with foil or spray with cooking spray, use olive oil to grease the inside of the mason jar lids, then arrange them onto the baking sheet. Fill each of the rings with about three tablespoons of the bun batter. Place the baking sheet into the preheated oven and allow the buns to bake for

15 minutes. The buns will be a light golden-brown color when they are done.

4. As the buns are baking, prepare your sandwich filling. Take a large frying pan, place it on your stovetop, and turn the heat to medium high. Allow the pan to heat up, then add your bacon slices. Cook for about 3 minutes on each side or until cooked to your desired crispness. Transfer the bacon to a plate lined with paper towels to catch the excess oil.

5. Drain the bacon grease from your skillet and return the skillet to the stove; turn the heat down to medium low.

6. In a small mixing bowl, crack your eggs and add in the sea salt and pepper. Gently beat the eggs with a fork then pour into the skillet. Fry the eggs for about 3 to 5 minutes on each side or until cooked to your preference. Turn the heat off.

7. Your buns should be done baking by the time your eggs and bacon are done. Allow the buns to cool for 5 minutes before trying to remove from the mason jar lids; use oven mitts to avoid burning your hands while removing the buns.

8. Now, it is time to assemble your sandwiches. Begin with one of the buns, then add on your eggs, bacon, and cheese slice. Top with another bun slice and enjoy.

*You can store leftover sandwiches in the freezer and reheat them in the microwave for an easy grab-and-go breakfast during your busy week. Ensure that the sandwiches are completely cooled before wrapping them individually in parchment paper or foil, then store them in a freezer bag. These sandwiches will stay fresh for up to six months. You can reheat them frozen—just be sure to wrap them in a paper towel before placing them in the microwave.

Cracker Barrel's Hashbrown Casserole

Potato hash browns aren't recommended on the keto diet, but this recipe substitutes cauliflower instead. You get a hearty breakfast that you can serve with eggs, bacon, or both.

Serving Size: ¼ of casserole

Prep Time: 5 minutes

Cook Time: 1 hour

Nutritional Information:

Calories 242

Carbs 6.5g

Fat 20g

Protein 9g

Ingredients:

- 1 ½ cups cauliflower (shredded)
- ½ cup sour cream
- ½ cup cheddar cheese (shredded, divided)
- ½ cup Monterey jack cheese (shredded, divided)
- ¼ cup mayonnaise
- ½ tablespoon onion powder
- ½ tablespoon bouillon powder
- ½ teaspoon Himalayan sea salt
- ½ teaspoon black pepper

Directions:

1. Begin by preheating the oven to 350 degrees Fahrenheit.

2. As the oven preheats, take a large mixing bowl and add ½ cup of the cheddar cheese and ½ cup of the Monterey Jack cheese. Next, add the cauliflower, sour cream, mayonnaise, onion powder, bouillon powder, sea salt, and black pepper. Use a baking spatula to gently mix everything together.

3. Pour the mixture into a greased 8x8 baking dish. Top with the remaining cheddar and Monterey Jack cheese, then place the baking dish into the oven and bake for 1 hour. The dish is done when the top is an irresistible golden-brown color.

4. Remove from the oven and divide into four equal portions.

Starbucks Cranberry Bliss Bars

This recipe includes a very small amount of molasses, which is one of those ingredients that some will argue whether it is keto. Rest assured! First, it is blackstrap molasses, which goes through an additional boiling process that removes excess traces of carbs but still provides you with the flavor. Second, it is such a small amount compared to the serving size that it has little if any effect on your carb intake. With that in mind, you can always take out the molasses and substitute maple extract in its place if you choose.

Serving Size: 1 bar

Prep Time: 10 minutes

Cook Time: 30 minutes

Nutritional Information:

Calories 110

Carbs 3g

Fat 10g

Protein 2g

Ingredients:

- 2 eggs
- 6 tablespoons butter (softened)
- ¼ cup almond flour
- ¼ cup coconut flour
- ¼ cup flax seed (ground)
- 1 cup cranberries (fresh)
- ½ cup erythritol
- ½ teaspoon stevia (pure)
- 1 teaspoon blackstrap molasses (pure)
- 1 teaspoon vanilla extract
- 1 teaspoon orange extract
- 1 teaspoon baking powder
- ¼ teaspoon Himalayan sea salt

For Frosting:

- 1 tablespoon butter (softened)
- 4 ounces cream cheese (softened)
- ½ cup erythritol (powdered)
- ½ tablespoon lemon extract

Directions:

1. Begin by preheating your oven to 350 degrees Fahrenheit and greasing an 8x8 baking dish with butter.

2. Next, take a large mixing bowl and mix the butter and erythritol until well combined.

3. Crack your eggs in a separate small bowl (to ensure you don't get any eggshells), then add them to your butter and sugar mixture. Add in the sea salt, orange extract, vanilla extract, and molasses and mix everything. Next, combine the almond flour, coconut flour, ground flaxseed, and baking powder into the mixture. Stir thoroughly and set to the side.

4. Take your cranberries and add them to a food processor with the stevia. Pulse for about 1 minute. Fold the cranberries into your other mixture then pour into your greased baking dish. Place your dish into the oven and bake for 30 minutes. The top should be a golden-brown color when done. Remove the dish from the oven to cool.

5. As your bars cool, make the frosting. In a medium-sized mixing bowl combine the butter, cream cheese, powdered erythritol, and lemon extract. Use a hand mixer to beat everything together until you have a fluffy consistency. Use a cake spatula to carefully spread the frosting over top of your bars. You want to do this slowly as the bars are still delicate and can crumble from too much pressure when frosting.

6. After frosting, place the baking dish into your refrigerator and chill for 30 minutes or until bars have cooled completely and are a bit firm.

Starbucks Egg Bites

These copycat egg bites are just as irresistible as the real thing, but they will cost you a lot less. Also, they are packed with protein and healthy fats that will help you refuel and keep you energized throughout your busy mornings.

Serving Size: 1 egg bite

Prep Time: 5 minutes

Cook Time: 20 minutes

Nutritional Information:

Calories 145

Carbs 1g

Fat 12g

Protein 9g

Ingredients:

- cooking spray
- 10 eggs

- ½ cup heavy whipping cream
- 1 cup cheddar cheese (shredded)
- 12 slices of bacon (cooked, crumbled)
- 1 red bell pepper (chopped)
- 1 teaspoon Himalayan sea salt
- 1 teaspoon black pepper

Directions:

1. First, move your oven rack to the lowest setting, preheat the oven to 350 degrees Fahrenheit, then spray a muffin pan with the cooking oil and set to the side.

2. In a blender add the eggs, heavy cream, cheddar cheese, bacon pieces, red bell pepper, sea salt, and black pepper. Blend for a few seconds so that everything is mixed together. Then fill each of your muffin slots ¾ of the way full. Place the muffin tray into the oven on the lowest rack and bake for 20 minutes.

3. Once the muffins have turned a light golden-brown color, remove them from the oven. Allow them to cool for a few minutes before servings.

Cinnabon's Cinnamon Rolls

Cinnamon rolls are one of my favorite breakfast treats. They fill your home with a sweet aroma that just brings a smile to your face. Unfortunately, the all-purpose flour, different sugars, and other ingredients mean it can be challenging to find a recipe that will work with your new lifestyle. Luckily, this recipe will allow you to indulge in these gooey breakfast pastries guilt free.

Serving Size: 1 cinnamon roll

Prep Time: 20 minutes

Cook Time: 15 minutes

Nutritional Information:

Calories 294

Carbs 4g

Fat 28g

Protein 7g

Ingredients:

- 1 egg
- 2 tablespoons butter (melted)
- ½ teaspoon cinnamon

- ½ cup almond flour
- 1 tablespoon coconut flour
- 1 ounce cream cheese
- 1 cup mozzarella cheese (shredded)
- 2 tablespoon erythritol
- 1 teaspoon baking powder
- 1 teaspoon vanilla extract
- ¼ teaspoon Himalayan sea salt

For Filling:

- 3 tablespoons butter (melted)
- 1 ½ teaspoon cinnamon
- 2 tablespoon erythritol

For Topping:

- 4 ounces cream cheese
- 2 tablespoon heavy cream
- 2 tablespoons butter (softened)
- ¼ cup erythritol (powdered)
- ½ teaspoon vanilla extract
- ¼ teaspoon almond extract

Directions:

1. In a small bowl combine 2 tablespoons of melted butter with ½ teaspoon of cinnamon. Mix with a fork, then take 3 small spring-form pans and grease the bottoms

and sides with the cinnamon butter. Set to the side until ready.

2. Take a large mixing bowl and add in the almond flour, coconut flour, baking powder, and sea salt. Mis thoroughly, then add the erythritol, vanilla extract, and eggs. Ensure everything is combined, then set to the side.

3. Next, you will need a microwave-safe bowl. Place the cream cheese and shredded mozzarella cheese into the bowl and heat in your microwave for 1 minute. Use a fork to mix together; the cheese should be completely melted.

4. Transfer the cheese mixture into the flour mixture. Use your hands to mix everything together nicely. This can take some time, usually about 2-3 minutes, until you have a suitable dough.

5. Once a dough has formed, separate into 3 equal portions and set them in the refrigerator for at least 5 minutes to firm up slightly.

6. Preheat the oven to 350 degrees Fahrenheit.

7. As the oven preheats and the dough chills, prepare your filling. Take a small mixing bowl and mix together the melted butter, cinnamon, and erythritol. Set to the side until ready.

8. Take your chilled dough and roll each piece out into a long log shape; they should be no more than a thumb-

width thick. Brush each log with your prepared filling mixture; save a little of the filling for later use.

9. Take your spring-form pan and lay the long side along the bottom, creating a spiral shape as you go. Brush the remaining filling mixture over the top of each swirled log and place in the oven. Bake the rolls for 15 minutes or until the tops have just started to turn a light golden brown.

10. As your rolls bake, prepare the topping. In a small mixing bowl, combine the cream cheese, heavy cream, softened butter, powdered erythritol, vanilla extract, and almond extract. Use a hand mixer to beat everything together until you have a smooth texture.

11. Once the rolls are done baking, remove them from the spring-form pans. Spread your topping over each one, cut them in half, and enjoy!

Krispy Kreme Doughnuts

Krispy Kreme doughnuts are known for being light and fluffy and having an irresistible sweet glaze. Unfortunately, they are not at all keto friendly, but this recipe will let you get your doughnut fix without throwing you off your weight loss journey. For this recipe, you will need a doughnut pan as this recipe bakes the doughnuts instead of frying them.

Serving Size: 1 doughnut

Prep Time: 10 minutes

Cook Time: 15 minutes

Nutritional Information:

Calories 171

Carbs 3g

Fat 14g

Protein 7g

Ingredients:

- 2 eggs
- ½ cup almond flour
- 2 tablespoons coconut flour
- ¼ cup vanilla almond milk (unsweetened)
- ¼ cup Swerve sweetener
- ¼ cup protein powder (keto friendly)
- 2 teaspoons baking powder
- 1 teaspoon vanilla extract
- ¼ teaspoon Himalayan sea salt

For Glaze:

- ¼ cup butter
- ¼ cup Swerve sweetener

- 1 teaspoon vanilla extract

Directions:

1. Begin by preheating your oven to 350 degrees Fahrenheit, then spray your doughnut pan with cooking spray and set to the side.

2. Next, take a large mixing bowl and add in your eggs, coconut milk, and vanilla extract. Beat together until the mixture begins to get frothy. Then, add in your almond flour, coconut flour, Swerve sweetener, protein powder, baking powder, and sea salt. Use a hand mixer to beat together all the ingredients until you have a smooth consistency. Your mixture should be dough-like but not as dry.

3. Transfer your dough into a piping bag (or you can use a Ziploc bag and cut one of the corners off). Fill each section of your doughnut pan with the dough about two-thirds of the way full. Then place your pan into the oven and bake for 15 minutes. The doughnuts should turn a light golden- brown color when they have baked all the way through. Remove the pan from the oven when done and allow the doughnuts to cool for at least five minutes before transferring them to a cooling rack.

4. As your doughnuts cool, prepare your glaze. In a small microwave-safe mixing bowl, add the butter, Swerve sweetener, and vanilla extract. Place the bowl in the

microwave for 30 seconds, then stir. If the butter does not melt completely or the sweetener has not completely dissolved, place it back in the microwave until everything has been thoroughly incorporated.

5. Once the doughnuts have cooled completely, dip each one into your glaze. Let the glaze settle on the doughnuts for a few minutes before enjoying.

Waffles House Waffles

Waffles are a treat at any time, but with the high carb content and added sugar, many people starting on the keto diet think that these breakfast treats are off limits. This recipe, however, is sugar and gluten free, making it keto approved! You'll need a waffle maker to enjoy these though, but even if you don't have one, you can make this batter and use it as a pancake recipe instead!

Serving Size: 1 waffle

Prep Time: 15 minutes

Cook Time: 25 minutes

Nutritional Information:

Calories 311

Carbs 2.5g

Fat 28g

Protein 8g

Ingredients:

- 5 eggs (separated)
- 3 tablespoons heavy cream
- ½ cup butter
- 4 tablespoons coconut flour
- 4 tablespoon erythritol (granulated)
- 1 teaspoon baking powder
- 2 teaspoon vanilla extract

Directions:

1. First, take a large mixing bowl and add in your egg yolks, coconut flour, granulated erythritol, and baking powder. Whisk everything together then slowly mix in your melted butter. Continue to whisk until you have a smooth consistency, then add in the heavy cream and vanilla extract. Whisk again until everything is well incorporated, set to the side.

2. Take a medium-sized mixing bowl and add in your egg whites. Take a hand mixer and beat the egg whites until they become nice and firm. When the whites are able to hold a peak, they are ready.

3. Use a large spoon to scoop some of the egg whites into the egg yolk mixture. Use a baking spatula to fold in egg

whites, then spoon in more; fold and continue until all the egg whites have been combined with the egg yolks. Don't overmix, you want the mixture to maintain some of the light fluffiness from the egg whites.

4. Take your waffle iron and turn it on. Use a spoon to fill the waffle maker and cook for about 5 minutes (cook time may vary depending on your model of waffle maker, double-check the user manual for approximate cook time). When the waffle is golden brown, it is done. Continues until all your waffle batter has been used.

Chapter 3: Lunch

Lunch is time you need to refuel your body with the right sources of energy. For many, these are often something they can order quickly and take back to their desks, so they can get back to work. Most grab-and-go lunch options from chain restaurants and fast-food places are high in carbs. This chapter focuses on putting a keto-twist on some of the most popular grab-and-go lunch choices that you can make with ease in your own home.

Wendy's Apple Pecan Salad With Chicken

This salad is filling and delicious, but apples are a no-no when you are on the keto diet. This rendition of Wendy's healthy lunch salad uses strawberries instead of the apples. You still get the summer-refreshing taste but without being thrown out of your ketosis.

Serving Size: ½ salad

Prep Time: 10 minutes

Cook Time: 10 minutes

Nutritional Information:

Calories 538

Carbs 5g

Fat 46g

Protein 24g

Ingredients:

- 2 tablespoons vegetable oil
- 2 chicken breasts
- 2 cups Romaine lettuce
- 1 cup spinach
- ¼ cup strawberries (sliced)
- ¼ cup cranberries (dried)
- 2 tablespoons pecans (chopped)
- ½ cup bleu cheese crumbles
- ¼ teaspoon parsley (dried)
- ¼ teaspoon garlic powder
- ¼ teaspoon Himalayan sea salt
- ¼ teaspoon black pepper

Directions:

1. Place a medium-sized skillet onto the stove and turn the heat to medium high. Add the oil to the skillet and allow it to get hot.
2. As the skillet is heating up, take a small mixing bowl and add the garlic powder, parsley, sea salt, and black pepper. Stir until well combined.

3. Take each of the chicken breasts and sprinkle on the garlic powder mixture on all sides.

4. Place your seasoned chicken breast into the skillet. Cook the chicken for five minutes then flip and cook for another five minutes. Once the internal temperature of the chicken has reached 165 degrees Fahrenheit, remove from the skillet and allow it to rest on a cutting board.

5. While the chicken is resting, prepare the rest of your salad. In a large salad bowl add the spinach, lettuce, strawberries, and cranberries. Toss everything together with salad spoons. Divide the salad into two equal portions and top each portion with half the pecans and bleu cheese.

6. Slice the chicken breast and place on top of your salad. Serve with your preferred keto-friendly salad dressing.

P.F.Chang's Chicken Lettuce Wraps

These lettuce wraps are my go-to lunch when I know I have a hectic day ahead of me. They are super easy to make ahead of time and quick to put together. The sauce, however, is what really makes these wraps standout.

Serving Size: ⅛ recipe

Prep Time: 10 minutes

Cook Time: 20 minutes

Nutritional Information:

Calories 155

Carbs 5g

Fat 5g

Protein 18g

Ingredients:

- 1 tablespoon avocado oil
- 1 pound chicken (ground)
- 1 head of butter lettuce
- 2 cups shiitake mushrooms (chopped)
- 3 green onions (sliced)
- ½ cup jicama (diced)
- 2 teaspoons onion powder
- ¼ teaspoon Himalayan sea salt
- ¼ teaspoon black pepper

For Sauce:

- 1 tablespoon sesame oil
- 2 cloves of garlic (minced)
- ½ teaspoon ginger (grated)
- ½ tablespoon erythritol (sweetener)
- 3 tablespoons coconut aminos

- 1 tablespoon apple cider vinegar
- 1 tablespoon almond butter

Directions:

1. Begin by making the sauce first. In a medium-sized mixing bowl, combine the sesame oil, minced garlic, grated ginger, erythritol, coconut aminos, apple cider vinegar, and almond butter. Use a whisk to vigorously mix everything together. Cover and store in your refrigerator until ready.

2. Now, take a large skillet and place it on your stove with a tablespoon of avocado oil in it. Turn the heat to medium, so the oil can get nice and hot. When the oil is heated, add in your ground chicken. Use a spatula to break it apart as it cooks. Allow the chicken to cook for 8 minutes or until it has all turned a light brown color.

3. Once the chicken has cooked add in the onion powder, sea salt, and black pepper. Stir everything together then add in the shiitake mushrooms, green onions, and jicama. Stir and cook for 5 minutes.

4. Once the mushrooms have softened, after about 5 minutes, pour your sauce over the top. Let the mixture simmer for 5 minutes then turn off the heat.

5. Take you butter lettuce and carefully remove the leaves. Place a leaf on a plate and spoon a quarter cup

of the chicken mixture in the center. Repeat until you have used up the chicken mixture. Serve and enjoy!

In-N-Out Burger

In-N-Out Burger is one of the best chain restaurants you can go to for an amazing burger. This recipe allows you to enjoy the same flavors and simply swaps out the traditional bun with a lettuce wrap. You can also use portobello mushroom caps if you want a sturdier burger.

Serving Size: 1 burger

Prep Time: 10 minutes

Cook Time: 10 minutes

Nutritional Information:

Calories 466

Carbs 5g

Fat 26g

Protein 48.5g

Ingredients:

- 1 ½ pounds lean ground beef
- 5 slices cheddar cheese

- 20 lettuce leaves
- 1 teaspoon Himalayan sea salt
- 1 teaspoon black pepper

*optional toppings:

- tomato slices
- onion slices
- pickle slices

For the Sauce:

- ½ cup mayonnaise
- 1 tablespoon sugar-free ketchup
- 1 teaspoon mustard paste
- 2 tablespoons pickles (diced)
- 2 teaspoon pickle juice
- ½ teaspoon paprika
- ½ teaspoon garlic powder
- ½ teaspoon Himalayan sea salt

Directions:

1. Begin by preparing the sauce. Combine the mayonnaise, sugar-free ketchup, mustard paste, diced pickles and pickle juice, paprika, garlic powder, and sea salt into a medium mixing bowl. Whisk everything together thoroughly, cover the bowl with plastic wrap, and store in the refrigerator until ready.

2. Next, you want to place a griddle pan or grill pan on your stove. Add a little bit of oil or cooking spray to the pan and turn the heat to medium, so it gets nice and hot as you prepare your patties.

3. In a large mixing bowl, add your ground beef, sea salt, and black pepper. Use your hands to mix everything together. Portion out the meat into five equal servings and roll them into a ball form then flatten slightly to form your patties. Place your patties onto your hot griddle and cook for 5 minutes on each side or until they turn a dark brown color.

4. When the burgers are done cooking, turn the heat off the stove and top the patties with your cheddar cheese slices.

5. To assemble your patties, lay two leaves of lettuce down first. Place your burger patty on the lettuce leaf, top with your favorite burger toppings, then take the sauce you prepared early and drizzle it over top. Place another two lettuce leaves on top and enjoy!

Buffalo Wild Wings Spicy Garlic Sauce Chicken Wings

Finding a good wing is challenging on its own. Trying to recreate one of your favorites doesn't have to be though. These wings are sweet and spicy and are great for lunch, as a snack, or when you are hosting a sports party. No one will even know they are eating something keto approved! You can also skip the sauce and simple season with your favorite spice.

Serving Size: ¼ recipe

Prep Time: 10 minutes

Cook Time: 50 minutes

Nutritional Information:

Calories 498

Carbs 4g

Fat 39g

Protein 30g

Ingredients:

- 2 ½ pounds chicken wings
- ½ teaspoon Himalayan sea salt

For Sauce:

- ¼ cup avocado oil
- ½ cup hot sauce
- 2 tablespoons garlic powder
- ¼ teaspoon cayenne pepper
- ½ teaspoon Stevia (liquid)

Directions:

1. Preheat your oven to 400 degrees Fahrenheit.
2. As the oven preheats, dry your wings using a paper towel then place them on a wire rack. Sprinkle them with sea salt and place them in the oven for 45 minutes.
3. After 45 minutes, turn your oven to broil and keep the wings in your oven for an additional 5 minutes, so they become nice and crisp.
4. As your wings bake, prepare the sauce. Combine the avocado oil, hot sauce, garlic powder, cayenne pepper, and liquid stevia in a blender. Blend until you have a smooth mixture then transfer to a large mixing bowl (the bowl needs to be large enough to hold all the wings as well).
5. Once the wings have come out of the oven, transfer them into the bowl with your sauce. Toss the wings so that they all get generously coated.

Chick-Fil-A's Chicken Nuggets

If you have kids and are trying to get them to eat a little healthier along with you, they are going to love these chicken nuggets. They have a nice crispy texture that kids love and that you will too. You can eat these as is or slice them up and place them on top of your favorite salad.

Serving Size: ⅓ recipe

Prep Time: 10 minutes plus 2 hours for chilling

Cook Time: 20 minutes

Nutritional Information:

Calories 261

Carbs 1g

Fat 9.5g

Protein 44.5g

Ingredients:

- 2 eggs
- 2 tablespoons heavy cream
- 1 pound chicken breast (cut into 1-inch pieces)
- 1 ½ cups panko breadcrumbs
- ½ cup pickle juice

- ½ teaspoon garlic powder
- ¼ teaspoon paprika
- ½ teaspoon Himalayan sea salt
- ¼ teaspoon black pepper

Directions:

1. Place your 1-inch cut chicken pieces into a sealable plastic bag. Pour in the pickle juice, seal the bag, and shake to ensure the chicken is well coated with the juice. Place the bag into the refrigerator for 2 hours.

2. When ready, preheat your oven to 425 degrees Fahrenheit. Then, line a baking sheet with parchment paper. Set the baking sheet to the side.

3. Take a medium-sized mixing bowl and combine the panko breadcrumbs, garlic powder, paprika, sea salt, and black pepper. Use a fork to mix everything together, then transfer to a sealable plastic bag and set to the side.

4. Take another medium-sized bowl and crack your eggs into it. Add in the heavy cream and beat together with a fork. Take your chicken pieces out of the refrigerator and transfer into the egg mixture. Make sure each piece gets well coated with the egg mixture.

5. Next, use tongs to transfer the chicken from the egg mixture to the plastic bag with the breadcrumbs. Give the bag a few shakes and gently press the breadcrumbs

into the chicken pieces. When the chicken looks evenly coated, remove them from the bag and place then on a roasting rack set on top of your lined baking sheet. Place the chicken into the oven and bake for 20 minutes.

6. Once the chicken is a crispy golden color remove from the oven and serve.

Mellow Mushroom's Pizza Holy Shiitake

Pizza is one of the most missed foods of those who just begin their keto diet, but it doesn't have to be! This copycat recipe is loaded with mushrooms that sit on top of an almond flour and cheese crust. The sauce is the key component that makes this pizza so delicious!

Serving Size: 1 square

Prep Time: 10 minutes

Cook Time: 25 minutes

Nutritional Information:

Calories 219

Carbs 3.5g

Fat 21g

Protein 6g

Ingredients:

- 3 tablespoons truffle oil
- 1 tablespoon butter (melted)
- 3 cups mozzarella cheese
- 4 tablespoons cream cheese
- 1 ½ cups almond flour
- 2 tablespoons baking powder
- 2 tablespoons Swerve sweetener
- 2 egg

Toppings:

- 1 cup mozzarella cheese (shredded)
- 2 cups baby bella mushrooms (sliced thin)
- ¼ cup oyster mushrooms (chopped)
- ¼ cup shiitake mushrooms (sliced)
- 1 sweet onion (diced)

Aioli Sauce:

- ¾ cup mayo
- 3 garlic cloves (minced)
- 3 tablespoons lemon juice
- ½ teaspoon Himalayan sea salt
- ½ teaspoon black pepper

Directions:

1. Begin by preheating your oven to 425 degrees Fahrenheit, then line a baking sheet with parchment paper and set to the side.

2. As the oven preheats, prepare your dough. Take a large, microwave-safe bowl and add in your 3 cups of mozzarella and cream cheese. Place the bowl in the microwave and heat for 1 minute. Stir and heat again for 30 seconds. Keep an eye on the mixture; you just want the cheese to melt and become properly incorporated, not burn.

3. Once the cheese is melted, add in the eggs, almond flour, baking powder, and sweetener. Begin to mix everything together using a fork; it may become easier to just use your hands once a dough begins to form.

4. Transfer the dough to your prepared baking sheet. Flatten the dough so that it stretches across the sheet or makes a rectangular shape. If the dough is too sticky, run your hands under cool water to help keep the dough from sticking to your fingers.

5. Once the dough is flattened out, use a fork to poke a few holes into the dough. Place the baking sheet into your oven and bake for 8 minutes. After 8 minutes remove your crust from the oven. If there are any bubbles in the crust, use a fork to pop them.

6. Take a small bowl and whisk together your truffle oil and melted butter. Then brush the mixture over the baked crust. Return the crust to the oven and bake for an additional 10 minutes.

7. As the crust continues to bake, prepare your toppings. Place a saucepan on your stove and turn the heat to medium. Add in your onions and sauté them until they turn a golden-brown color. Add your baby bella, shiitake, and oyster mushrooms to the pot. Allow the mushrooms to cook for 3 minutes, then turn off the heat.

8. Once your crust has turned a nice golden-brown color, remove it from the oven. Sprinkle your mozzarella cheese over the top then pour the mushroom mixture over the cheese. Return the pizza to the oven and bake for 3 more minutes or until the cheese has melted. Remove the pizza from the oven and allow it to cool slightly.

9. As the pizza cools, prepare your aioli sauce. Take a small mixing bowl and stir together the mayonnaise, minced garlic cloves, lemon juice, sea salt, and black pepper. Drizzle your sauce over the pizza then cut into 16 equal squares and serve.

Jimmy John's Unwich

What is great about this copycat recipe is that it doesn't need much tweaking since it is already mostly keto friendly. This is a quick and easy to put together lunch idea that you can make a part of your regular meal plan on the keto diet.

Serving Size: 1 sandwich

Prep Time: 5 minutes

Nutritional Information:

Calories 422

Carbs 4g

Fat 32g

Protein 18g

Ingredients:

- 2 slices turkey breast
- 1 slice provolone cheese
- 2 large iceberg lettuce leaves
- 1 tomato (sliced)
- 1 cucumber (sliced)
- ½ avocado (sliced)
- 1 teaspoon mayonnaise

- 1 teaspoon yellow mustard

Directions:

1. Place your lettuce leaves flat on a plate. Then, layer a slice of your turkey, then provolone, and another slice of turkey. Next, add 3 tomato slices, 5 cucumber slices, and your avocado slices. Top with mayonnaise and mustard.

2. Begin to wrap the lettuce like you would a burrito. Fold in the ends so you have a square/rectangular shape, the start at one of the unfolded ends and begin to roll everything together. Secure with a toothpick or pick up and enjoy!

Wendy's Chili

Chili is just one of those great comfort foods you want to have a go-to recipe for to create on your own. This recipe uses keto-friendly ingredients that taste identical to the chili you stop at the Wendy's drive-through to quickly grab on a cold brisk day. Feel free to top this chili with sour cream, shredded cheddar cheese, or green onion.

Serving Size: ⅛ recipe

Prep Time: 10 minutes

Cook Time: 1 hour 45 minutes

Nutritional Information:

Calories 362

Carbs 3g

Fat 11g

Protein 53g

Ingredients:

- 3 pounds ground beef
- 2 teaspoons erythritol (granulated)
- ⅔ cups celery (diced)
- ½ cup red bell pepper (diced fine)
- ½ cup green bell pepper (diced fine)
- 1 ½ cups yellow bell pepper (diced fine)
- 1 cup tomatoes (diced)
- 1 ½ cups tomato juice
- 1 15-ounce can crushed tomatoes in purée
- 3 tablespoons Worcestershire sauce
- 3 tablespoons chili powder
- 1 teaspoon garlic powder
- 1 teaspoon cumin
- ½ teaspoon oregano (dried)
- 1 teaspoon Himalayan sea salt
- ½ teaspoon black pepper

Directions:

1. Take a large stockpot and place it on your stove; turn the heat to medium high to warm. Add your ground beef into the pot and allow it to cook for about 10 minutes or until it has all properly cooked and is a deep brownish color. Stir the meat regularly to avoid any large clumps of meat from forming. Once the ground beef has cooked, drain the excess oil, leaving about 2 tablespoons in the pot.

2. Add the onions, celery, red, green, and yellow bell pepper, and diced tomatoes. Stir and let the peppers cook for 5 minutes.

3. Next, pour in the tomato juice, crushed tomatoes, and Worcestershire sauce. Stir and allow the liquid to simmer for 3 minutes.

4. Add in the chili powder, garlic powder, cumin, oregano, sea salt, and black pepper to the pot. Stir, reduce the heat to medium, cover, and allow everything to cook for 1 hour.

5. After an hour stir, uncover, and cook for another 30 minutes over medium-low heat.

6. Turn off the heat and allow the chili to sit for about 10 minutes then ladle into bowls, top with your favorite toppings, and enjoy!

Are you enjoying this book? If so, I'd like to hear your thoughts: please leave a short review on Amazon. Thank you.

Chapter 4: Dinner

Eating out at a nice restaurant is difficult when on the keto diet but not impossible if you stick with salads and steaks. You don't have to go out to enjoy some of your favorite restaurant dishes. The recipes in this chapter will guide you to recreating flavorful dinner options that you and your family will love. Many of the recipes you will find in this chapter can also be used for lunch options any day of the week.

Long John Silver's Batter-Dipped Fish

That golden crust on Long John Silver's will hook you almost every time. When I was younger, we used to wait until just about closing and ask for all the leftover fried bits of dough. With this recipe, I can relive my childhood whenever I like. The batter in this recipe also works well with chicken strips.

Serving Size: ⅙ recipe

Prep Time: 5 minutes

Cook Time: 10 minutes

Nutritional Information:

Calories 559

Carbs 2g

Fat 43g

Protein 37g

Ingredients:

- 4 cups vegetable oil (for frying)
- 2 pounds cod (cut into three-inch pieces)
- 16 ounces club soda
- ¼ cup ground flaxseed
- 2 cups almond flour
- ½ teaspoon paprika
- ½ teaspoon onion salt
- ½ teaspoon baking soda
- ½ teaspoon baking powder
- 1 teaspoon Himalayan sea salt
- ¼ teaspoon black pepper

Directions:

1. First, take a deep frying pan and fill it with the 4 cups of oil. Turn the heat to medium to preheat the oil.
2. As the oil heats, combine the almond flour and ground flaxseed with the paprika, onion salt, baking soda, baking powder, sea salt, and black pepper into a medium-sized mixing bowl. Whisk everything together so it is well incorporated, then add the club soda. Whisk again until the batter has a foamy consistency.

3. Take your cod pieces and dip them into your batter. Ensure that each piece is coated completely then carefully place them into the preheated oil. Do not overcrowd your pan or your fish will not cook evenly. If needed, fry in two batches. Allow the fish to fry for 5 minutes. The fish should have a nice golden color and will begin to float on the oil when done.

4. Remove the fish from the oil using a slotted spoon and transfer them to a plate lined with paper towels to catch the excess oil.

5. Serve with your favorite side!

Olive Garden's Steak Gorgonzola Alfredo

If you need a great romantic dinner recipe, this is your recipe. The steaks are flavorful, and you won't miss the alfredo noodles with the zucchini noodle substitute. This meal is sure to impress and will keep you on track with your weight loss goals.

Serving Size: ¼ recipe

Prep Time: 20 minutes plus 20 minutes chill time

Cook Time: 25 minutes

Nutritional Information:

Calories 413

Carbs 6g

Fat 28g

Protein 30g

Ingredients:

- 1 pound of steak medallions
- 1 tablespoon balsamic vinegar
- ½ teaspoon Himalayan sea salt
- ½ teaspoon black pepper
- 5 zucchinis
- 4 ounces gorgonzola crumbles
- ¼ cup sun-dried tomatoes

For the Sauce

- 2 cups heavy cream
- 1 stick of unsalted butter
- 1 cup parmesan cheese
- 2 cups spinach
- ¼ teaspoon nutmeg
- ¼ teaspoon Himalayan sea salt
- ¼ teaspoon black pepper

Directions:

1. Begin by marinating your steaks. First, sprinkle them with the Himalayan sea salt and black pepper, then place them in a sealable bag. Add the balsamic vinegar to the bag and seal. Place the steaks in your refrigerator for at least 30 minutes before cooking

2. As the steaks marinate, place a large pot of water on your stovetop and turn the heat to medium high. Then take a spiralizer and create your "fettuccine noodles" using the zucchini. You can also use a vegetable peeler to peel thicker zoodles if you do not have a spiralizer. When done, add them to your boiling pot of water for 3 minutes. Then, drain the water and transfer your zucchini noodles to a plate lined with a paper towel, so the excess water can drain off.

3. Next, take a large skillet and place it on your stove. Turn the heat to medium and allow it to heat up. Remove your steak medallions and place them into the hot skillet. Allow them to cook on each side for about five minutes. The thickness of the steak will determine how long you need to cook the steaks. Steaks that are a little over two inches should reach a medium cook in 5 minutes per side. If you prefer your steak more rare, cook for a shorter amount of time. For those who like a more well-done steak, cook for two minutes longer.

Your steaks should have a nice brown color to them when they are done.

4. Once the steaks have reached your desired cook time, remove them from the skillet and place them on a plate, then cover them with aluminum foil to rest. Keep in mind your steaks will still continue to cook even though you have removed them from the skillet.

5. As the steaks rest, you want to make your sauce. Place a medium-sized saucepan on your stove and turn the heat to medium. Add in the butter and heavy cream. Once the butter has begun to melt, add in your spinach. Allow the spinach to cook down; this should only take about 5 minutes. Once the spinach has wilted, add in the parmesan cheese, sea salt, and black pepper. Stir, reduce heat to medium low and allow the sauce to thicken slightly for about 5 minutes.

6. Once the sauce is done, turn off the heat. Transfer your zucchini noodles to a large bowl and pour the sauce over top (leave a little sauce in the saucepan to top your steaks with). Toss the zucchini noodles with the sauce so that everything gets nicely coated. Add in the gorgonzola cheese, but reserve some to top your steaks with during plating. Toss everything one more time.

7. Now it is time to assemble the plate! Place a small portion of the zucchini noodles on your dinner plate, place a steak medallion on top of the noodles, and top

with the dried tomatoes, gorgonzola crumbles, and a little drizzle of your leftover sauce.

Chipotle's Chipotle Pork Carnitas

This delectable dish is easy to make and can be used in a number of ways. I like to make this big batch and freeze half of it for a meal later on in the month. To serve, top your favorite southwestern salad with the pulled pork, wrap in large lettuce leaves, or serve with your favorite keto-friendly tortilla!

Serving Size: 1/12 recipe

Prep Time: 5 minutes

Cook Time: 4 hours and 10 minutes

Nutritional Information:

Calories 317

Carbs .5g

Fat 14.5g

Protein 43g

Ingredients:

- 1 cup water

- 2 tablespoons avocado oil
- 4 pounds pork roast
- 1 teaspoon thyme
- 2 teaspoon juniper berries
- 1 teaspoon Himalayan sea salt
- ½ teaspoon black pepper

Directions:

1. Begin by preheating your oven to 300 degrees Fahrenheit.

2. Next, take a Dutch oven pot, place it on your stove, and turn the heat to medium. Add the avocado oil to the pot.

3. As the pot heats, take your pork roast and sprinkle it with the sea salt. Then place the roast into the Dutch oven pot and brown the sides for a minute on each side.

4. Turn the heat off on the stove once the roast has browned. Add the water, thyme, juniper berries, and black pepper to the pot, then cover. Place the pot into your preheated oven and allow the roast to cook for 3 ½ hours. Turn the roast every half hour so that the flavors really penetrate into all areas of the meat.

5. Remove the roast from the oven after 3 ½ hours (keep the oven turned on), allow it to rest for 10 minutes, then use two forks to pull the meat apart. Once all the meat

has been pulled, place the pot back into the oven for 30 minutes.

6. Remove the pot and enjoy!

KFC Fried Chicken and Coleslaw

Yes! Even on the keto diet, you can enjoy crispy fried chicken. This meal is great for any night of the week, and the leftovers make great lunches for the next day. If you like your chicken extra crispy, you can add a cup of panko breadcrumbs or crushed pork rinds to your seasoning mixture.

Serving Size: ⅙ recipe

Prep Time: 30 minutes plus 4 hours chill time.

Cook Time: 20 minutes

Nutritional Information:

Calories 376

Carbs 5g

Fat 29g

Protein 17g

Ingredients:

- 8 cups olive oil

- 2 pounds chicken drumsticks
- 1 ½ cups whey protein powder
- 4 tablespoons white vinegar
- 3 tablespoons heavy cream
- 2 cups almond milk (unsweetened)
- 2 eggs

Seasoning:

- 1 teaspoon celery salt
- 1 teaspoon ginger powder
- 2 teaspoon garlic salt
- 4 teaspoons paprika
- ¼ teaspoon oregano (dried)
- ½ teaspoon thyme (dried)
- 1 teaspoon mustard powder
- 1 tablespoon black pepper
- 1 teaspoon Himalayan sea salt

For the Coleslaw:

- ¾ cup mayonnaise
- 2 cup carrots (shredded)
- 3 cups white cabbage (shredded)
- 1 cup purple cabbage (shredded)
- ¼ cup white wine vinegar
- ½ teaspoon garlic powder
- ¼ teaspoon celery salt

- ⅓ cup sour cream
- ½ teaspoon mustard
- ½ teaspoon Himalayan sea salt

Directions:

1. First, prepare your seasoning by mixing all ingredients under the seasoning section in the ingredient list into a small bowl. Divide the mixture in half and set to the side.

2. Next, take a large bowl and pour in the almond milk, white vinegar, heavy cream, and eggs. Whisk everything together thoroughly. Then add in half of the seasoning mixture and whisk until you have a nice smooth mixture.

3. Take your chicken drumsticks and place them into a sealable plastic bag or a large airtight container. Pour in the almond milk mixture and ensure that all the chicken is well coated. Seal the bag or place the lid on your container and place it into your refrigerator for at least 4 hours.

4. When your chicken is done marinating, take a large skillet and pour in the olive oil. Turn the heat to medium high and allow the oil to become hot. This should take about 15 minutes, and the temperature of the oil should be 325 degrees.

5. Once the oil is at the appropriate temperature, take a rimmed plate and spread out the rest of the seasoning onto it. Take your marinated chicken and coat each piece with the seasoning mixture, then carefully place the chicken into the hot oil. Allow each drumstick to cook for 20 minutes; the internal temperature should be 165 degrees Fahrenheit. When your chicken is done, remove it from the pan and place it on a plate lined with paper towels to catch the excess grease.
6. Serve with a side of coleslaw (see below).

For the Coleslaw:

1. In a large salad bowl or mixing bowl, combine the shredded carrots and white and purple cabbage. Toss everything together and set to the side.
2. Take a smaller mixing bowl and combine the mayonnaise, white wine vinegar, celery salt, sour cream, mustard, and sea salt. Whisk so that everything is thoroughly mixed.
3. Pour your mayonnaise mixture over your cabbage mixture and toss until everything is well coated. Place the bowl, covered, into your refrigerator and chill for 30 minutes before serving.

Longhorn's Parmesan Crusted Chicken With Mashed Potatoes

Potatoes are considered a high-starch vegetable, so instead of traditional mashed potatoes, this recipe is served with a cauliflower mash. You can also use the same seasoning and marinade on salmon steaks for something different.

Serving Size: 1 chicken breast

Prep Time: 20 minutes plus 30 minutes chill time.

Cook Time: 20 minutes

Nutritional Information:

Calories 557

Carbs 10g

Fat 42g

Protein 31g

Ingredients:

- 2 tablespoons avocado oil
- 4 chicken breasts (boneless, skinless)
- 1 cup panko breadcrumbs
- ¾ cup parmesan cheese
- ¾ cup provolone cheese

- ¼ cup heavy cream
- 1 teaspoon onion powder
- 2 teaspoons garlic powder
- 1 teaspoon dill (dried)
- 1 teaspoon parsley (dried)
- 1 teaspoon chives (dried)
- 2 teaspoon Himalayan sea salt
- 2 teaspoon black pepper

For the Marinade:

- ½ cup avocado oil
- 2 garlic cloves (minced)
- 1 teaspoon lemon juice
- 3 tablespoons Worcestershire sauce
- 1 teaspoon white vinegar
- ½ teaspoon black pepper
- ½ cup keto ranch dressing (see recipe in Chapter 8)

Directions:

1. First, you want to prepare your chicken. Take each breast and use a meat tenderizer mallet. I also prefer the old-fashioned way of just using a rolling pin and pounding each breast so they are about ¾" thick. Then season each breast with ½ teaspoon of sea salt and black pepper. Next, take a small mixing bowl to whisk up your marinade. Combine the ½ cup avocado oil,

minced garlic cloves, lemon juice, Worcestershire sauce, white vinegar, and keto-friendly ranch dressing. Whisk everything thoroughly. Place your chicken breast into a sealable plastic bag and pour the marinade sauce into the bag. Seal the bag and give it a good shake to ensure all the breasts are nicely coated. Place the bag into your refrigerator for at least 30 minutes.

2. Once the chicken has marinated, place a large skillet on your stovetop with 2 tablespoons of avocado oil in it. Turn the heat to medium to allow the oil to heat up. Remove your chicken from the bag and carefully place them into the hot skillet. Cook each side of the chicken for 5 minutes then transfer them to a baking dish to rest.

3. As your chicken is resting, preheat your oven to 450 degrees Fahrenheit.

4. Next, you need a small microwave-safe mixing bowl and add your heavy cream, parmesan cheese, provolone cheese, onion powder, dill, parsley, and chives. Mix everything together and then place the bowl into your microwave and heat for 30 seconds. Remove and stir, microwave for another 15 seconds, stir, and repeat until you have a smooth, creamy mixture. Pour this mixture over your chicken breasts

and place your baking dish into the oven. Allow the chicken to bake for 5 minutes.

5. While the chicken bakes, take a small bowl and combine the panko breadcrumbs and garlic powder. Stir everything together. Once the chicken has been in the oven for 5 minutes, remove the dish and sprinkle the breadcrumbs over top. Place the dish back in the oven and bake for another 5 minutes or until the breadcrumbs have turned a lovely golden-brown color.

6. Remove from the oven and serve with cauliflower rice (see below).

To Make Cauliflower Rice:

Ingredients:

- 2 tablespoons olive oil
- 1 cauliflower head (should yield 4 cups of "rice")
- ½ teaspoon Himalayan sea salt
- ¼ teaspoon black pepper

Directions:

1. Begin by creating your rice. You can do this by chopping the cauliflower into pieces and then adding them to a food processor and pulsing, or you can use a grater to grate the cauliflower into small rice bits. Once you have rice, sprinkle your sea salt and black pepper over top and gently mix everything together.

2. Take a large skillet and place it on your stove with the olive oil in it. Turn the heat to medium high and allow the oil to get hot.

3. Place your riced cauliflower into the skillet and cook for 5 minutes, stirring occasionally. The cauliflower should be soft and not mushy. Then turn off the heat and enjoy!

Red Lobster's Shrimp Scampi with Cheddar Bay Biscuits

Shrimp scampi is a simple dish to make, and this recipe can be deliciously paired with any number of vegetable noodles or added to a large salad. Red Lobster's cheddar biscuits are truly one of a kind, and everyone I know says they go there just for them. This copycat recipe of the cheddar, fluffy biscuits is a great side for any meal. The best thing about this meal is that it takes little to no time to have something healthy prepared for dinner.

Serving Size: ¼ recipe

Prep Time: 10 minutes

Cook Time: 25 minutes

Nutritional Information:

Calories 591

Carbs 6g

Fat 39g

Protein 45g

Ingredients:

For the Scampi

- 1 ¼ pounds shrimp (peeled, tail removed, deveined)
- 2 garlic cloves (minced)
- 2 scallions (sliced)
- 4 tablespoons butter (unsalted)
- ⅓ cup parmesan cheese (shredded)
- ¼ cup lemon juice
- ¼ cup chardonnay
- ¼ cup parsley (chopped)
- ¼ teaspoon red pepper flakes

For the Biscuits

- 1 ½ cups almond flour
- 2 eggs
- 1 ½ teaspoons garlic powder (separated into 1 and then ½ teaspoon)
- 1 tablespoon baking powder
- ½ cup cheddar cheese (shredded)

- ½ cup sour cream
- 6 tablespoons butter (unsalted, melted, separated into 4 and then 2 tablespoons)
- 1 tablespoon parsley (minced)
- ½ teaspoon Himalayan sea salt

Directions:

1. Place a large skillet on your stove and turn the heat to medium with the butter in it. Allow the skillet to heat up for a few minutes until the butter has melted then add the garlic. Cook the garlic for 1 minute so that it becomes a light golden color.
2. Take the shrimp and add them to the skillet. Let them cook for 3 minutes. Sprinkle the red pepper flake over the shrimp, flip, and cook for another 3 minutes.
3. Once the shrimp have turned a pink color, pour in the lemon juice and chardonnay. Allow everything to simmer for 2 minutes then turn off the heat.
4. Add the scallion and parsley to the skillet. Stir everything together and top with the parmesan cheese.
5. Serve over top of your favorite vegetable noodles like zucchini or spaghetti squash.

To make the Biscuits:

1. Preheat your oven to 450 degrees Fahrenheit, then grease a muffin pan with oil and set to the side.

2. In a large mixing bowl, add your almond flour, 1 teaspoon garlic, baking powder, and salt. Use a fork to mix everything together, set to the side.

3. In a small bowl, crack your eggs then pour in four tablespoons of the melted butter and the sour cream. Beat the eggs and sour cream until well incorporated, then add to your flour mixture. Stir your ingredients together until you have a smooth batter, then fold in your cheddar cheese.

4. Take your muffin pan and fill each section with the batter. Place your pan into the oven and bake for 10 minutes. The biscuits should be a light golden color when they are done. Ensure the inside of the biscuits are done by inserting a wooden toothpick into one. If it comes out clean, they are done. If there is batter coated on the toothpick, put them back into the oven for a few more minutes.

5. As the biscuits bake, take a small bowl and add the remaining 2 tablespoons of butter and ½ teaspoon of garlic powder. Stir together until the garlic powder has dissolved then add your parsley. Once the biscuits have been removed from the oven, brush each one with your butter and parsley mixture then serve warm.

P.F.Chang's Beef and Broccoli

The flavors of this rendition of P. F. Chang's popular beef and broccoli dish are incredible. If you haven't tried coconut aminos before, it is about to become a staple in your kitchen. It is a keto-friendly soy sauce alternative that doesn't have all the sugar and preservatives. After you've tried it in this recipe, you are bound to want to use it more.

Serving Size: ¼ recipe

Prep Time: 10 minutes plus 30 minutes of chill time.

Cook Time: 15 minutes

Nutritional Information:

Calories 264

Carbs 3g

Fat 7.5g

Protein 43g

Ingredients:

- 2 tablespoons avocado oil
- 1 pound steak (cut to ¼-inch slices)
- 1 head of broccoli (florets)
- 2 scallions (chopped)

- 2 garlic cloves (minced)
- ¼ teaspoon ginger (dried)
- 2 teaspoons sesame seeds
- 2 tablespoon water

For Marinade:

- 1 tablespoon avocado oil
- 2 tablespoons coconut aminos
- 1 garlic clove (minced)
- ¼ teaspoon ginger (dried)
- 1 teaspoon crushed red pepper
- ¼ teaspoon baking soda
- ½ teaspoon Himalayan sea salt

For Sauce:

- 1 tablespoon fish sauce (low carb)
- 2 tablespoons coconut aminos
- 2 teaspoons sesame oil
- ½ teaspoon black pepper

Directions:

1. First, make the sauce. Take a small mixing bowl and combine the fish sauce, coconut aminos, sesame oil, and ground black pepper. Stir everything together thoroughly then set to the side until ready.

2. Next, prepare the marinade. In another large mixing bowl, combine the avocado oil, coconut aminos, minced garlic, dried ginger, crushed red pepper, baking soda, and sea salt. Whisk everything together thoroughly. Then add the sliced steak into the bowl. Toss the steak around so that it is all well coated then cover and place in the refrigerator for at least 30 minutes.

3. As the meat is marinating, take a microwave-safe bowl and add your broccoli florets with the 2 tablespoons of water. Place the bowl in the microwave and heat on high for 3 minutes, then set to the side.

4. When the meat has been marinated for long enough, take a large skillet and place it on your stove. Turn the heat to medium and add in the avocado oil. Allow the oil to heat for a few minutes then add the minced garlic. Cook the garlic for 1 minute. Then turn the heat to high and add in your steak pieces. Allow the steak to cook for 2 minutes on each side.

5. Take your broccoli florets and add those to the skillet along with the ginger. Then pour over your sauce and give everything a stir. Reduce heat and allow the sauce to simmer for 5 minutes.

6. Toss in your scallion and sesame then serve!

Outback Steakhouse Charcoal Ribeye

Outback Steakhouse is of course known for its perfectly seared steaks, and the ribeye is one of the most popular steaks on the menu. This recipe makes a few changes without losing the flavors so that you can enjoy this dinner any night of the week.

Serving Size: ⅛ recipe

Prep Time: 5 minutes

Cook Time: 15 minutes

Nutritional Information:

Calories 139

Carbs 2g

Fat 4g

Protein 27g

Ingredients:

- 4 ribeye steaks (cut to 1 ½-inch thick slices, fat trimmed)
- 1 teaspoon turmeric powder
- 2 teaspoons paprika
- 1 teaspoon chili powder
- ½ teaspoon thyme (dried)

- ½ teaspoon garlic powder
- ½ teaspoon onion powder
- ½ teaspoon ground mustard
- ½ teaspoon cumin (ground)
- ½ teaspoon ancho chili pepper (ground)
- ½ teaspoon Himalayan sea salt
- ½ teaspoon black pepper

Directions:

1. Begin by placing a grill pan on your stove or turn your outdoor grill on to medium-high heat. Brush your grill pan or outdoor grill with oil.
2. Next, take a small bowl and combine the turmeric powder, paprika, chili powder, thyme, garlic powder, onion powder, ground mustard, cumin, ancho chili pepper, sea salt, and black pepper. Use a fork to thoroughly mix all the ingredients together.
3. Take each of your steaks and season them generously with your spice mixture on both sides. Then place the steaks onto your grill. Cook for 5 minutes on each side for a medium-cooked steak. Remove the steaks from the grill when they are at your desired doneness and cover them with foil to rest for 5 minutes.
4. When the steaks have rested, slice the steaks and serve on top of your favorite salad or along with your favorite roasted vegetables.

Chili's BBQ Baby Back Ribs

Ribs are a summer staple where I'm from. We tend to grill them up a few times a month. The key to making your favorite Bar-B-Que dishes keto friendly is to choose the right sauce. Be sure to use a low-carb version with no added sugar. You can omit it from this recipe if you prefer a dry rub rack of ribs.

Serving Size: ⅓ rack of ribs

Prep Time: 10 minutes

Cook Time: 3 hours

Nutritional Information:

Calories 483

Carbs 2.5g

Fat 41g

Protein 24g

Ingredients:

- 2 tablespoons avocado oil (divided)
- 2 racks baby back ribs (remove membrane)
- ½ cup BBQ sauce (low carb)
- 1 teaspoon paprika
- 1 teaspoon garlic powder

- 1 teaspoon onion powder
- 1 teaspoon ground mustard
- ½ teaspoon cinnamon
- ½ teaspoon celery salt
- ½ teaspoon cayenne pepper
- 1 teaspoon Himalayan sea salt
- 1 teaspoon black pepper

Directions:

1. First, turn your oven to 275 degrees Fahrenheit.
2. Next, prepare your seasoning rub by combining the paprika, garlic powder, onion powder, ground mustard, cinnamon, celery salt, cayenne pepper, sea salt, and black pepper in a small mixing bowl. Use a fork to stir everything together.
3. Take your racks of ribs and generously rub your seasoning mix all over them. Leave a little of the seasoning mix aside for later.
4. Place your ribs on a rimmed baking sheet, cover, and seal with aluminum foil. Place the baking sheet into your preheated oven and allow the ribs to cook for 2 ½ hours. You'll be tempted to check on them because the smell will fill your home, but resist the urge to peek at them.
5. After 2 ½ hours, take the baking sheet from the oven and uncover. Sprinkle the leftover seasoning mix over

top and pour the BBQ sauce over top. Return the baking sheet into the oven for another 30 minutes.

6. The ribs should be a rich dark-red color when done. After removing them from the oven. allow them to rest for 10 minutes before serving.

Chapter 5: Soups

Soups are one of those comfort foods that make you feel warm inside. This chapter is dedicated to providing you with a more versatile number of soup recipes, so you don't always have to have the same chicken and vegetables while you are working towards a healthier lifestyle. Here, you will learn how to easily create a bowlful of savory and satisfying soup perfect for dinner or lunch.

Pappadeaux's Crawfish Bisque

If you are lucky enough to have access to fresh crawfish, then this is a must-try recipe. Don't be intimidated by the cleaning or shelling process. This bisque utilizes the extra flavor in its rich broth.

Serving Size: ¼ recipe

Prep Time: 15 minutes

Cook Time: 2 hours

Nutritional Information:

Calories 275

Carbs 2.5g

Fat 18g

Protein 25g

Ingredients:

- 4 cups water
- 1 tablespoon olive oil
- 1 ½ pounds of crawfish
- ¼ cup tomatoes (chopped)
- ¼ cup onions (chopped)
- ¼ cup green bell pepper (chopped)
- 1 ½ cups heavy cream
- ½ tablespoon tomato paste
- ½ teaspoon paprika
- ¼ teaspoon cayenne pepper

Directions:

1. Take a large pot filled with water and place it on your stove. Turn the heat to high to bring to a boil. Once the water is boiling, add your crawfish and boil for 15 minutes. Then turn off the heat and allow the crawfish to cool for 15 minutes.
2. Take the crawfish and separate the tail meat, set the shells and heads in a bowl to use for the stock later, and put the meat in a bowl to store in the refrigerator until you are ready for it.

3. Once you have separated the meat from the shells, place a large saucepan on your stove with the olive oil in it and turn the heat to medium heat. Add the heads and shells from the crawfish to the saucepan along with the cayenne pepper and paprika. Allow everything to sauté over medium heat for 5 minutes. Then, add the water and bring everything to a boil. Once the liquids are boiling, lower the heat to medium low and simmer for 30 minutes.

4. After 30 minutes, strain the liquid from the pan into a medium-sized bowl using a cheesecloth. Discard the shells and heads, then pour the liquid back into the saucepan. Turn the heat to medium low and add in the tomato paste, heavy cream, chopped tomatoes, onions, and green bell peppers. Allow the vegetables to simmer for 1 hour then add in the crawfish meat. Simmer everything for another 15 minutes then serve.

Panera Bread's Broccoli Cheddar Soup

The broccoli and cheddar soup from Panera Bread is probably one of its most popular soups. It's rich and creamy and simply just delicious. This recipe takes inspiration from Panera's soup but simplifies it and makes it keto friendly.

Serving Size: ⅙ recipe

Prep Time: 10 minutes

Cook Time: 25 minutes

Nutritional Information:

Calories 295

Carbs 5g

Fat 24g

Protein 13g

Ingredients:

- 1 tablespoon olive oil
- 3 ½ cups low-sodium chicken or vegetable broth
- ½ cup heavy cream
- 2 cups broccoli (chopped)
- 1 cup carrots (shredded)
- ½ cup white onions (diced fine)
- 4 ounces of cheddar cheese (shredded)
- 4 ounces gouda cheese
- 4 ounces cream cheese
- ¼ teaspoon black pepper

Directions:

1. Get a large saucepan and place it on your stovetop. Add the olive oil to the pan and turn the heat to medium.

Allow the pan to heat for a few minutes then add your onions and sauté them for about 5 minutes.

2. Add the cream cheese to the pan and stir frequently to allow the cheese to begin to melt. Slowly pour in the heavy cream, then add in the gouda and shredded cheddar cheese. Continue to stir for 3 minutes.

3. Add your chopped broccoli to the pan along with the chicken or vegetable broth. Allow the broth to simmer for 5 minutes, then add in the carrots and black pepper. Lower the heat to medium low, cover, and let the soup cook for 10 minutes.

4. After 10 minutes, you can take half the soup and transfer it to a blender. Blend on high until you have a smooth consistency, then transfer back into the pan and stir until everything comes together. This will give you a slightly thicker but smoother soup. If you want a chunkier soup, then just serve hot after it has cooked for 10 minutes in the previous step.

Carrabba's Sausage and Lentil Soup

While lentils are nutritious, they tend to have a higher amount of net carbs, which doesn't make them keto friendly. This recipe takes out the lentils and swaps in eggplant and cauliflower for a great spin-off on the widely known Carrabba's signature sausage and lentil soup.

Serving Size: ⅙ recipe

Prep Time: 10 minutes

Cook Time: 1 hour and 20 minutes

Nutritional Information:

Calories 338

Carbs 4.5g

Fat 26g

Protein 17g

Ingredients:

- 2 tablespoons olive oil
- 1 pound Italian sausage
- 4 cups low-sodium vegetable broth
- 1 cup white onion (diced)
- 1 cup cauliflower (florets, riced)
- ½ cup eggplant (diced small)
- 2 cups tomatoes (diced)
- 3 garlic cloves (minced)
- ½ cup celery (diced)
- ½ cup carrots (diced)
- 2 teaspoons Italian seasoning

Directions:

1. Take a large soup or stock pot and place it on your stove with the 2 tablespoons of olive in it. Turn the heat to medium high and allow the oil to heat up for a few minutes, then add your onions, garlic, celery, and carrots to the pot. Let the vegetables cook for about 5 minutes, until the onions are translucent.

2. Lower the temperature of your stove to medium and add the Italian sausage to the pot. Let the sausage cook thoroughly for about 10 minutes.

3. Once the sausage is cooked all the way through, pour in the vegetable broth, diced tomatoes, eggplant, and Italian seasoning. Cover the pot, reduce the heat to medium low, and allow everything to simmer for 45 minutes.

4. Add the cauliflower to the pot and cook for another 15 minutes.

5. Serve hot and store leftovers in the refrigerator for up to 5 days.

Applebee's Tomato Basil Soup

Tomato soup is just a classic. While it is quite easy just to reach for a can of the condensed stuff, you will want to reconsider while on keto. Most store-bought canned soups contain high amounts of added sugars and preservatives. This recreation of Applebee's tomato basil soup will show you that making soup from scratch is not just easy, but the resulting product has more flavor and is better for you.

Serving Size: ⅙ recipe

Prep Time: 10 minutes

Cook Time: 50 minutes

Nutritional Information:

Calories 180

Carbs 5g

Fat 13g

Protein 10g

Ingredients:

- 1 tablespoon butter (unsalted)
- 4 ounces cream cheese
- 4 tablespoons parmesan cheese (grated)
- 2 cups chicken broth
- 6 tomatoes (skin removed, crushed or use 1 14-ounce can of whole tomatoes)
- ¼ cup red onions (diced fine)
- 1 garlic clove (minced)

- ½ tablespoon basil (dried)
- ½ teaspoon oregano (dried)
- ½ teaspoon Himalayan sea salt
- ¼ teaspoon black pepper

Directions:

1. Place a large soup pot on the stove with the butter in it. Turn the heat to medium to melt the butter.

2. Once butter is melted, add the diced red onions, minced garlic, basil, and oregano. Allow the onions to cook until they become soft, about 5 minutes.

3. Turn the heat to medium low and add in your cream cheese. Use a whisk to break up the cream cheese and eliminate any clumps.

4. Pour in the chicken broth, then add in the tomatoes, parmesan cheese, sea salt, and black pepper. Whisk everything together thoroughly, then cover and allow the soup to simmer for 30 minutes. Stir occasionally.

5. After 30 minutes, remove the lid. Use an immersion blender to purée the soup (you can also use your blender and work in batches, then return the purée back into the pot). Simmer for another 5 minutes then ladle into soup bowls and enjoy.

Chapter 6: Desserts

Dieting doesn't mean you don't get to have dessert. When you go out to eat, you always have a little room for dessert, and when you are cooking at home, this can still be enjoyed. This chapter will introduce you to baking while on the keto diet. You will learn how to make some of the most irresistible desserts that you won't have to feel bad about enjoying.

Chili's Molten Lava Cake

The gooey overflowing fudge-like center and the most delicate cake exterior will make you think you are eating something you shouldn't be while on the keto diet. When you use this recipe there will be nothing to worry about.

Serving Size: 1 cake

Prep Time: 10 minutes

Cook Time: Nutritional Information:

Calories 172

Carbs 3.5g

Fat 14g

Protein 8g

Ingredients:

- 4 eggs
- 6 tablespoons heavy whipping cream
- 6 tablespoons erythritol (sweetener)
- 8 tablespoons cocoa powder (unsweetened)
- 1 teaspoon baking powder
- 2 teaspoons vanilla extract (unsweetened)

Directions:

1. Set your oven to 350 degrees Fahrenheit and grease the inside of four ramekins with butter then set to the side.
2. Nest, take a medium-sized mixing bowl and add the cocoa powder, baking powder, and erythritol. Whisk everything together thoroughly and set to the side.
3. In another medium-sized mixing bowl, crack your eggs and beat them with a fork until frothy. Then add in the vanilla extract and heavy whipping cream. Use a blender to evenly blend together.
4. Combine the egg mixture in the bowl with your cocoa powder. Blend until you have a smooth consistency. Take a spoon and fill your ramekins with the batter. Then, place your ramekins into the oven and bake for 12 minutes. The tops of your cakes should be firm but still moist.
5. Remove the ramekins from the oven and allow them to cool for a few minutes. When ready to serve, place a

plate over the top of the ramekin and flip it upside down so that your cake comes out. You can top each with keto-friendly ice cream, whipped cream, or indulge in them just as they are.

Wendy's Frosty

This is a delicious, keto-friendly version of the irresistible chocolate frosty from Wendy's. You can easily leave out the cocoa powder for a vanilla frosty or add in some frozen strawberries for a strawberry frosty.

Serving Size: ½ recipe

Prep Time: 15 minutes plus 45 minutes of chill time

Nutritional Information:

Calories 169

Carbs 2.5g

Fat 17g

Protein 2g

Ingredients:

- ¾ cup heavy cream
- 2 tablespoons erythritol

- 1 ½ tablespoons cocoa powder (unsweetened)
- ¾ teaspoon vanilla extract
- ⅛ teaspoon Himalayan sea salt

Directions:

1. You will need a large mixing bowl to begin with. Pour in the heavy cream, erythritol, cocoa powder, vanilla extract, and salt. Use a hand mixer to blender all the ingredients together until you have a smooth and thick mixture. You should see stiff peaks begin to form after you have been blending for about 5 minutes.

2. Transfer the mixture into an airtight, sealable bag. Place it in your freezer for at least 45 minutes.

3. Once frozen, cut one end of the bag and squeeze your frosty into a small cup or serving dish with a straw or spoon and enjoy!

Starbucks Lemon Bread

This is a refreshing dessert that tastes just like the scrumptious lemon bread you'll find tempting you at the local store display window. What is even better about this copycat recipe though is its low-carb, low-sugar content makes it a versatile delight. You can enjoy this as a dessert or even grab a slice for breakfast!

Serving Size: 1 slice

Prep Time: 10 minutes

Cook Time: 1 hour

Nutritional Information:

Calories 117

Carbs 1g

Fat 11.5g

Protein 2.5g

Ingredients:

- 6 eggs
- ¾ cup butter (melted)
- 2 tablespoons cream cheese (softened)
- 2 tablespoons heavy whipping cream
- ½ cup coconut flour
- 1 ½ teaspoons baking powder
- ½ cup erythritol (granulated)
- 1 teaspoon vanilla extract
- 2 lemons (zest- reserve 1 teaspoon for glaze)
- 4 teaspoons lemon juice
- ½ teaspoon Himalayan sea salt

For Glaze:

- ½ tablespoon heavy whipping cream (more if needed)
- 2 tablespoons erythritol (granulated)
- 1 teaspoon lemon zest
- 2 teaspoons lemon juice

Directions:

1. Begin by preheating the oven to 350 degrees Fahrenheit, then take a bread pan and line it with parchment paper and set to the side.

2. As the oven preheats, take a medium-sized mixing bowl and crack the eggs into it. Add in the granulated erythritol, cream cheese, heavy whipping cream, vanilla extract, baking powder, and sea salt. Use a hand mixer to beat everything together.

3. Next, add the melted butter, coconut flour, lemon zest, and juice to the egg mixture. Mix again until well combined. Then, pour the mixture into your bread pan. Place the pan into the oven and bake for 1 hour. When the top is just about to turn golden, it should be done, but double check by inserting a toothpick into the center and seeing if it comes out clean. If there is still batter on the end, allow it to bake for another 5 minutes, until the toothpick comes out clean.

4. As the bread bakes, prepare the glaze. In a medium-sized mixing bowl combine the heavy whipping cream,

erythritol, lemon zest, and lemon juice. Use your hand mixer to blend everything together until you have a smooth glaze. If it seems to be too thick, add another small splash of heavy whipping cream until it thins out slightly.

5. Once the bread is done baking, remove it from the oven. Carefully lift it out of the pan, using the parchment paper to easily free it, and transfer it to a cooling rack. Then, take your glaze and pour it over top. Use a baking spatula to spread the glaze out evenly over top and allow for some of it to drip down the side. Allow the bread to cool enough so the glaze solidifies, then slice and serve.

Cinnabon Cookies

Cinnabon is known for its irresistible cinnamon buns, but they also have a number of other sweet treats that are amazing. Their cookies are just as fluffy as their cinnamon buns. This takes those delicious cookies and transforms them into a keto delight! They are fluffy and chewy, and you won't even miss the ones from Cinnabon.

Serving Size: 1 cookie

Prep Time: 30 minutes plus 40 minutes chill time

Cook Time: 7 minutes

Nutritional Information:

Calories 65

Carbs 2g

Fat 6g

Protein 1.5g

Ingredients:

- 3 tablespoons butter (softened)
- 1 egg white
- ¾ cup almond flour
- 1 tablespoon erythritol (liquid)
- 1 tablespoon Splenda
- ¼ teaspoon baking powder
- ¼ teaspoon xanthan gum
- ¼ teaspoon Himalayan sea salt

For the Filling:

- ½ tablespoon butter
- ½ teaspoon cinnamon
- 2 tablespoons erythritol (granulated)

For the Cream Cheese Frosting:

- 1 tablespoon coconut oil

- 2 tablespoons cream cheese
- ⅛ teaspoon vanilla extract
- 2 tablespoons erythritol (granulated)

Directions:

1. First, prepare your dough by combining the almond flour, Splenda, baking powder, xanthan gum, and sea salt in a medium-sized mixing bowl. Use a fork to stir everything together thoroughly. Then add in the softened butter, erythritol liquid. and egg whites. Mix everything together until a dough begins to form. This can take a little effort as it will start off looking really dry. You'll be tempted to add extra moisture into it but be patient; the more you stir it, the more dough-like it will become.

2. Once you have a dough, roll it into a log form and cover it with plastic wrap. Place it in the refrigerator for at least 20 minutes.

3. As your dough chills, prepare your filling ingredients. Take a small mixing bowl and combine the cinnamon and the granulated erythritol. Use a fork to stir the two ingredients together. Then take your tablespoon of butter and place it into a microwave-safe bowl. Place it in the microwave for 15 seconds or until completely melted. Set to the side until needed.

4. Once your dough has chilled for 20 minutes, take it out and unwrap it. Lay a piece of parchment paper down on your countertop and roll the dough out into a rectangular shape. Roll it on the thicker side, about ½ inch thick.

5. Take your melted butter and brush it over top of the rolled dough, then sprinkle your cinnamon and sweetener mixture over top.

6. Begin at one end of the dough and roll it over to the other side. The dough may break or crack, which is fine. Once you have rolled the dough, press it together so you form a long square block out of it. Wrap it in plastic wrap again and place it back into the refrigerator for 20 more minutes.

7. When the 20 minutes is just about up, begin to preheat your oven to 350 degrees Fahrenheit. Then line a baking sheet with parchment paper and set to the side.

8. Remove your dough from the refrigerator and cut it into 8 equal squares. Place them on the lined baking sheet and put them into the oven. Bake the cookies for about 7 minutes. The tops and sides should be a light brown color when they are done. Remove them from the oven and transfer them to a cooling rack. They will feel soft once they first come out of the oven. but once they have set, they will firm up. Allow the cookies to cool for 10 minutes.

9. As the cookies are cooling, prepare your frosting. Take a small microwave-safe mixing bowl and combine your coconut oil and cream cheese. Place the bowl in the microwave for 30 seconds. Take it out of the microwave and stir the mixture together. Next, add in your vanilla extract and granulated erythritol. Whisk together until you have smooth glaze-like frosting.

10. Once the cookies have cooled down, drizzle your cream cheese frosting over top and enjoy!

Cheesecake Factory's Classic Cheesecake

The classic cheesecake from the Cheesecake Factory is absolutely divine. It is everything you want in a cheesecake: rich, creamy, and delicious. Unfortunately, it also includes a number of ingredients that you want to avoid while on the keto diet. This recipe gives you a worthy replacement that is just as indulgent but healthier.

Serving Size: 1/12 cheesecake

Prep Time: 15 minutes plus 24 hours chill time

Cook Time: 1 hour

Nutritional Information:

Calories 348

Carbs 3g

Fat 34g

Protein 8g

Ingredients:

For Crust:

- ¾ cup almond flour
- 3 tablespoons flaxseed (ground)
- 6 tablespoons butter (melted)
- ⅓ cup walnuts (chopped fine)
- ⅓ cup erythritol
- ¼ teaspoon Himalayan sea salt

For Filling:

- 3 eggs
- 1 ½ cups erythritol
- 24 ounces cream cheese (softened)
- 8 ounces sour cream
- 2 teaspoons lemon juice
- 2 teaspoons vanilla extract
- ¼ teaspoon Himalayan sea salt

Directions:

1. Begin by preheating your oven to 375 degrees Fahrenheit.

2. Next, start by making the crust. In a large mixing bowl, stir together the almond flour, ground flax seeds, finely chopped walnuts, and the sea salt.

3. In a small mixing bowl, combine the melted butter and erythritol. Pour the butter mixture into the flour bowl and mix thoroughly. Take a 9-inch spring-form pan and pour your crust into it. Use your hand to evenly spread the dough across the bottom of the pan, pressing gently. Place the pan into your oven and bake for 10 minutes. The crust should turn a light golden color. Remove from the oven and allow it to cool.

4. Lower the temperature of your oven to 325 degrees.

5. As your crust cools, place your cream cheese into a large mixing bowl. Use a hand blender or stand-alone mixer, set to the lowest setting, to beat the cream cheese until it is fluffy. Then add in the erythritol and continue to mix until you have a rich, creamy texture. Now add the eggs one at a time. Next add in the sea salt, lemon juice, and vanilla extract. Beat together until everything is nicely combined then add in the sour cream. Once everything has been mixed thoroughly, pour the mixture over your cooled crust. Then place the pan into the oven and bake for 50 minutes. After 50 minutes, check to see if the top has turned a light golden-brown color. If the top has not started to brown, leave in for another 5-10 minutes. Once the top has

turned a light brown, turn off the oven and keep the cheesecake in it for at least an hour with the oven door slightly opened. This will reduce the risk of the cheesecake cracking when it cools too fast.

6. After an hour, remove the pan from the oven and allow it to come to room temperature, then place it in the refrigerator for 24 hours before serving.

Chapter 7: Drinks

While water is the best for you to drink when you are drinking to lose weight, it can get quite boring. This chapter provides you with a number of refreshing and delightful drinks from a number of popular restaurants. These recipes are a great alternative to the juices, pops, and coffees you might be used to reaching for.

Orange Julius's Orange Julius

An Orange Julius is a refreshing drink that is delicious at any time of year. Unfortunately, the orange juice and other citrus juices used in this drink are not keto friendly. This recipe utilizes orange extract and cream cheese to give it the citrus, tangy, and smooth flavors that make the original so delightful. After one sip, you won't believe you aren't drinking the real thing.

Serving Size: ½ recipe

Prep Time: 5 minutes

Nutritional Information:

Calories 325

Carbs 2.5g

Fat 34g

Protein 3g

Ingredients:

- ⅔ cup heavy cream
- 2 tablespoons cream cheese
- 3 tablespoons erythritol
- 1 ½ teaspoons lemon juice
- 1 ½ teaspoons orange extract
- 1 ½ cups crushed ice

Directions:

1. Pour the heavy cream into your blender and blend on high until it begins to thicken.
2. Add in the cream cheese, erythritol, lemon juice, orange extract, and crushed ice. Blend for another minute until the mixture becomes smooth and creamy.
3. Pour into two equal servings and drink away!

McDonald's Shamrock Shake

Each year when McDonald's announces the return of the Shamrock Shake, people flock to the nearest one and go crazy! With this easy to make copycat recipe, you won't have to wait or skip this refreshing treat. The spinach powder is what gives it that recognizable green color, but it also packs a nutritional punch you won't get with the original.

Serving Size: ½ recipe

Prep Time: 5 minutes

Nutritional Information:

Calories 354

Carbs 7g

Fat 31.5g

Protein 3g

Ingredients:

- ¾ cup almond milk (unsweetened)
- ¼ cup low-carb keto vanilla ice cream
- 2 teaspoons spinach powder
- ¼ teaspoon mint extract

Directions:

1. Pour the almond milk into a food processor then add in the ice cream, spinach powder, and mint extract. Secure the lid and pulse for 1 minute until you have a smooth mixture.
2. Pour the shake into two equal portions and enjoy.

Starbucks Coffee Frappuccino

When you want a fancy coffee but want to avoid all the extra milk, creamer, and sugar, this is your recipe. It perfectly mimics Starbucks popular frappuccinos that will cool you down on a warm day any time.

Serving Size: ½ recipe

Prep Time: 5 minutes

Nutritional Information:

Calories 182

Carbs 1g

Fat 15g

Protein 1g

Ingredients:

- ½ cup heavy cream
- ½ cup cold brewed coffee
- ¾ teaspoon erythritol
- 1 ½ cups ice

Directions:

1. Pour the heavy cream, cold-brewed coffee, and erythritol into a blender. Add your ice and pulse for

about a minute until you have a thick and smooth mixture.

2. Pour into two equal servings. You can top with keto-friendly whipped cream and low-carb caramel sauce if you desire.

Starbucks Iced Matcha Latte

This recipe is a great option for those who love their green tea. The almond milk and vanilla syrup tone down the bitterness of the matcha powder for a perfectly balanced iced tea.

Serving Size: ½ recipe

Prep Time: 5 minutes

Nutritional Information:

Calories 200

Carbs 4g

Fat 16g

Protein 5g

Ingredients:

- 2 tablespoons avocado oil
- 2 cups almond milk (unsweetened)

- 2 tablespoons vanilla syrup (sugar free)
- 2 teaspoons matcha powder
- 2 cups ice

Directions:

1. Pour the almond milk, avocado oil, and vanilla syrup into the blender, then add the matcha powder. Secure the lid and pulse three times. Uncover, add your ice, and place the lid back on. Pulse for 1 minute until the mixture is nice and smooth.
2. Pour your iced matcha latte into two equal portions and enjoy!

Chapter 8: Sauces and Dressings

Keto-friendly sauces and dressing are hard to find. Even when you come across one in the grocery store that says low carb or no sugar added, there's a good chance these labels are misleading. To avoid consuming something you want to avoid, this recipe will provide you with an array of sauces and dressing.

McDonald's Big Mac Special Sauce

The secret sauce on the McDonald's Big Mac is an infamous sauce that many try to replicate. While most other recipes call for excess sugar, this one gives you the same flavors without unnecessary carbs. Now you'll be able to make your own Big Mac (minus the bun) at home whenever you want!

Serving Size: ⅙ recipe

Prep Time: 5 minutes

Nutritional Information:

Calories 138

Carbs 1g

Fat 16g

Protein 0g

Ingredients:

- ½ cup mayonnaise
- 1 teaspoon erythritol
- 1 teaspoon dill pickle juice
- 1 tablespoon white onion (diced)
- 2 tablespoons pickles (diced)
- 1 tablespoon keto ketchup

Directions:

1. Combine the mayonnaise, erythritol, pickle juice, diced onions, pickles, and keto ketchup into a small mixing bowl. Use a fork or spoon to mix everything together thoroughly. Transfer to an airtight container and store in your refrigerator until ready to use.

Chipotle Sweet and Smoky Vinaigrette

This sweet and spicy dressing is the perfect topping for any salad. You can also drizzle it over roasted vegetables or use it as a marinade for chicken, steaks, or fish.

Serving Size: 1/32 recipe

Prep Time: 5 minutes

Nutritional Information:

Calories 103

Carbs 3g

Fat 11.5g

Protein 1g

Ingredients:

- 1 ½ cups avocado oil
- ½ cup red wine vinegar
- ⅓ cup erythritol (liquid)
- 1 tablespoon adobo sauce
- 1 teaspoon oregano (dried)
- 1 teaspoon garlic powder
- 1 teaspoon cumin
- 1 tablespoon Himalayan sea salt
- 1 ½ tablespoons black pepper
- 1 tablespoon water

Directions:

1. In your food processor, add the red wine vinegar, erythritol, adobo sauce, oregano, garlic powder, cumin, sea salt, black pepper, and water. Secure the lid and pulse for 30 seconds until the mixture is nice and smooth.

2. After 30 seconds of pulsing, slowly pour in the oil as you continue to blend. Once all the oil is added, pulse for another 30 seconds.

3. Transfer the dressing to an airtight container and use as needed.

Olive Garden's Angry Alfredo Sauce

This alfredo sauce adds a little kick to traditional sauces. It has a little bit of spice that isn't overwhelming but will wake up your taste buds. You can easily put this sauce together even on your busiest of days and have a delicious and healthy meal ready in a little over ten minutes (if you are making your own noodles), but it will seem like you spent all day in the kitchen.

Serving Size: ¼ cup

Cook Time: 10 minutes

Nutritional Information:

Calories 345

Carbs 2.2g

Fat 32g

Protein 13.5g

Ingredients:

- 1 cup heavy cream
- ½ cup butter
- ½ cup parmesan cheese
- ¼ teaspoon red pepper flakes
- ½ teaspoon garlic powder

Directions:

1. Place a saucepan on your stove and turn it to medium heat. Add the butter, and when it has melted completely, pour in the heavy cream. Stir the mixture until the cream begins to bubble then add the parmesan cheese. Allow the sauce to thicken, stirring occasionally, this should take about 5 minutes.

2. Lower the heat and add in the red pepper flakes and garlic powder. Stir, and simmer the sauce for another minute. Ladle on top of your favorite veggie noodles and enjoy!

Keto Ketchup

Ketchup is one of the most popular condiments for so many dishes. Store-bought ketchup, unfortunately, is loaded with added sugars and carbs. This recipe allows you to enjoy the traditional flavors of ketchup but cuts out all the extra sugars and uses mushrooms as a thickening instead of the flour or cornstarch many other homemade recipes call for. You can store this ketchup in your refrigerator for up to a month once it has cooled completely and is in an airtight container.

Serving Size: 1 tablespoon

Prep Time: 10 minutes

Cook Time: 45 minutes

Nutritional Information:

Calories 10

Carbs 2.5g

Fat .5g

Protein .5g

Ingredients:

- 3 pounds (around 24) plum tomatoes (quartered)
- ¼ cup mushrooms (diced fine)
- ¼ cup white vinegar
- ¼ teaspoon allspice
- ¼ teaspoon onion powder
- ¼ teaspoon garlic powder
- 2 teaspoons erythritol (granulated)

Directions:

1. Place a large saucepan on your stove and turn the heat to medium.
2. Add the quartered tomatoes, diced mushrooms, vinegar, allspice, onion powder, garlic powder, and erythritol to the saucepan. Give everything a stir, cover, and cook for 30 minutes.
3. After 30 minutes, uncover, transfer to a blender, and blend until you have a smooth consistency. Return the mixture to the saucepan, lower the temperature to medium low, and simmer for another 10 minutes. Stir occasionally. Then turn off the heat.
4. Allow the ketchup to cool completely. Transfer to an airtight container and use as needed.

Ranch Dressing

Ranch dressing is one of the most popular dressings, but it is typically made with milk and sweeteners that you are trying to cut out of your diet. This recipe gives you the ideal alternative that is tangy and delicious. What's great about this dressing is that you can modify it to satisfy your taste buds. Want your ranch to have more of a dill flavor? Just add a little more.

Serving Size: 1/12 recipe

Prep Time: 5 minutes

Nutritional Information:

Calories 156

Carbs .5g

Fat 16.5g

Protein .5g

Ingredients:

- 1 cup mayonnaise
- ½ cup sour cream
- ¼ cup almond milk (unsweetened)
- 2 teaspoons lemon juice
- 2 teaspoons parsley (dried)
- 1 teaspoon dill (dried)
- 1 teaspoon chives (dried)
- ½ teaspoon garlic powder
- ½ teaspoon onion powder
- ½ teaspoon Himalayan sea salt
- ¼ teaspoon ground black pepper

Directions:

1. In a mason jar or medium mixing bowl, add the mayonnaise, sour cream, lemon juice, parsley, dill,

chives, garlic powder, onion powder, sea salt, and black pepper. Whisk everything together.

2. Slowly add in the almond milk. If you want to have a thicker dressing for dipping, add less almond milk. For a thinner dressing for salads, add slightly more almond milk.

3. Cover with a mason jar lid or transfer to an airtight container and store in your refrigerator for up to two weeks.

Conclusion

Dieting does not have to mean deprivation. While the keto diet can be viewed as a restrictive diet, what it really is, is just a new way to approach what you eat. You don't have to dread never getting to enjoy a dessert or your favorite meals you loved ordering when you would go out to eat. You don't have to struggle to come up with exciting meals that will encourage you to stick to your goals.

This book has provided you with a basic understanding of how to transition to a low-carb, high-fat diet. We have discussed the first steps you can take to make the keto diet not just another diet, but a new way of eating. When you first understand where you are starting, you know what direction to go in. The action steps in the first chapter help you achieve just that.

You have been provided with some easy-to-make meals that won't throw you off your weight loss goals. Unlike when I first attempted the keto diet, you are already set up for success! You don't have to go back and forth trying to find the right ingredient to substitute. The recipes in this book do that for you already!

The recipes in this book provide you with the first steps to learning how to cook the right way while on the keto diet. You have been introduced to a number of new ingredients that allow you to still enjoy your favorite meals. These recipes can become your go-to for breakfast on the go and quick lunches, and even your kids will willingly sit down and eat dinner!

Now that you have everything you need to get started and have success on the keto diet, it is up to you to make the commitment and actually take the first step. I encourage you to start today! Create a meal plan that swaps out those unhealthy carbs and introduces more vegetables and lean meats. Choose one breakfast, lunch, and dinner recipe from this book to try this week. Don't be intimidated by the newness of this diet. Don't focus on what you will have to give up because, for the most part, there is almost always a keto-friendly alternative or copycat recipe that will make you realize this diet isn't as restrictive as you may have first believed.

Once you just get started and try new recipes, you will quickly make the keto way of eating a part of your lifestyle. And when you do, you will reap the benefits of a healthier and satisfying life. This is just the first step on your journey to a happier and healthier lifestyle that will continue to give back for years to come. Now it is up to you to just take the first step. Good luck and happy eating!

Did you enjoy this book? Please let me know your thoughts by leaving a short review on Amazon! Thanks again.

Other books by Lisa Ramsey

Copycat Recipes Cookbook: LINK

From a 5-star chef mom or dad whipping up a 6 course dinner, to a novice student that's just trying to comfort their midnight Taco Bell cravings, we've all needed a little nudge in the right direction when it comes to mastering perfect home cooked meals!

The best dishes truly are made with love, and these copycat recipes of all of your favorite dishes – from breakfast, to appetizers, to pastas, Japanese, Mexican, to some good ol' barbecue style ribs and everything in between, you'll *love* these simple and easy homemade recipes for you to treat yourself and your loved ones to!

From fast food to cuisines from all around the world, you can now travel the world from the comfort of your home! You'll be sure to find some tantalizing, mouth-watering and heavenly recipes that will get yours and your guests' tummies growling for more.

82 Copycat Recipes offers a compilation of a wide variety of dishes – many that may be familiar to you, but also some new recipes that you never thought to try or cook! That's the beauty of this list – it offers dishes from all over, covering all diets and perfect meals for different times of the day!

You're guaranteed to find a few of your favorite meals to whip up, but also expect to explore a few new dishes that may be a new fan-favorite on your weekly meals! And best of all? These dishes will prove how cost-friendly home-cooked meals are.

References

Baker, K. (2020). Keto copycat recipes: Delicious, quick, healthy, and easy to follow cookbook for making your favorite restaurant dishes at home the ketogenic way. Amazon.com Services LLC.

The easiest keto waffles - award winning recipe - 2.5g net carbs. (n.d.). Ditch the Carbs. www.ditchthecarbs.com/keto-waffles/

Keller, K. (2020) Keto copycat recipes cookbook: Easy, vibrant, and classic restaurant favorites adapted into the low carb, high fat ketogenic diet! Amazon.com Services LLC.

Lauren. (2020, January 1). Keto copycat In N' Out burger. Bonappeteach. www.bonappeteach.com/keto-copycat-in-n-out-burger/#.XQKLQ9NKg6U

Lina. (2019, January 2019). Make your own Jimmy John's Unwich at home! Hip2Keto, hip2keto.com/recipes/keto-copycat-jimmy-johns-unwich-recipe/

Lyndsey. (2018, June 12). Keto donuts recipe {Krispy Kreme copycat}. Momma Fit Lyndsey. www.mommafitlyndsey.com/keto-donuts/

Marley. (2018. December 20). Love Wendy's famous chili? Try our keto copycat recipe! Hip2Keto. hip2keto.com/recipes/wendys-chili-keto-copycat-recipe/

Mawer, R. (2018, July 30). The ketogenic diet: A detailed beginner's guide to keto. Healthline. www.healthline.com/nutrition/ketogenic-diet-101#17

Maya. (2017, August 21). Low carb keto ranch dressing recipe (quick & easy). Wholesome Yum. www.wholesomeyum.com/recipes/low-carb-keto-ranch-dressing/

Sammysamgurl. (2018, January 31). Cinnabon keto cookies w/ cream cheese frosting. Mouthwatering Motivation. mouthwateringmotivation.com/2018/01/31/cinnabon-keto-cookies-w-cream-cheese-frosting/

Sugar-free instant pot ketchup + video. (n.d.). Ditch the Carbs. www.ditchthecarbs.com/sugar-free-instant-pot-ketchup/

Trenum, K. (2019, March 30). Keto lemon bread recipe: Perfectly moist & delicious. Kasey Trenum. kaseytrenum.com/keto-lemon-bread-recipe-perfectly-moist-delicious/

Made in the USA
Columbia, SC
17 November 2020